"Love's Resurrection: A Spiritual Journey through Marriage, Divorce and Remarrying the Same Man is a must read whether you're already married, considering marriage or involved in a committed relationship. *Love's Resurrection* brings out the importance of prioritizing our relationship with our Higher Power as our steps are ordered to sustain healthy marriages/committed relationships. In addition to our Spirituality, other resources (marital/family therapists, retreats, etc.) help us strengthen our interactions. By identifying healthy marriages/healthy relationships as a top priority, we will see our community heal and our children thrive. Thanks to the author for doing an excellent job of telling the truth about current reality conflicts in marriages and also for identifying Higher Power solutions that are "fail-proof." Once I picked up this beautiful memoir, I couldn't put it down."

—Chandra Mathews-Smith, MSW, LISW
VP New Business Development,
BeechAcres Parenting Center

"Reading this book and reliving these experiences makes me so proud of my wife. She has truly made a conscious effort to help both of us identify—and correct—what made our first marriage fail. The transformation she reveals in *Love's Resurrection* will be an inspiration to both husbands and wives, and will make their marriages great like God has made ours."

—Andre Harper, Husband

Love's Resurrection

A spiritual journey through
marriage, divorce, and
remarrying the same man

Dominique,
may God continue to add
new life to your love!

Kristin
Harper

A true story by

KRISTIN R. HARPER

*Love's Resurrection: A Spiritual Journey through Marriage,
Divorce, and Remarrying the Same Man*

Published by Wheatmark®
610 East Delano Street, Suite 104
Tucson, Arizona 85705 U.S.A.
www.wheatmark.com

International Standard Book Number: 978-1-60494-120-3
Library of Congress Control Number: 2008927382

To Ms. Kelley.

I will never forget the advice you gave me years ago:
"Let the bird go, and if it's really yours, it will fly back
to you."
God gave us a second chance, and I am so grateful.
Thank you for raising such a wonderful son.
I promise that I will love and treasure him for the rest
of my days.

Contents

Foreword

Feeling trapped in a failed marriage, Kristin R. Harper laments all the choices she wishes she hadn't made and decides that her only way out is to speak the truth in love.

Love's Resurrection: A Spiritual Journey through Marriage, Divorce and Remarrying the Same Man is a page turner. In my counseling of married couples, I constantly encounter couples who have been unfaithful to each other, but I have never had one who has admitted infidelity to God.

Kristin felt trapped and desperately wanted a way out of her marriage. She felt she was being destroyed physically, emotionally, and spiritually. The operative word here is *feel.* Not long ago, we held the mistaken belief that we had little or no control over the way we felt. It was natural to feel a certain way, we believed. So we allowed ourselves to let our dominant feelings rule our lives. We now know better. Today we have undeniable clinical evidence that we create our feelings by the way we choose to think. Kristin knew that if things were going to get better for her, she would have to start looking at herself first. Right choice.

Kristin Harper has written a must-read for all those who are feeling trapped in a failed relationship. She has shown us how to make the necessary choices in order to free ourselves. I'm not in a failed marriage, but after reading this book, I'm freer. *Wow!* I'm closer to God because spiritual infidelity is the worst kind. I highly recommend this book to all who may need to reset their priorities in the wrong place.

—Rev. Damon Lynch Jr.
Pastor, New Jerusalem Baptist Church
Cincinnati, Ohio

Acknowledgments

There are countless people to whom I would like to show appreciation, not only in the birth of this book, but also in my development from a girl into a woman.

– To God, who makes all things possible and works out everything for my good.

– To my husband, Andre. I thank God every day that he gave me a second chance to agape you. You are my best friend, lover, confidante, and life-long partner. Thank you for allowing me to bare my soul—and the details of our relationship—in order to help women and men become free. You are special beyond words!

– To my beautiful daughter. You were brought into this world with heavenly purpose and faith. Your boundless energy has brought our family overflowing joy and youthfulness, and you leave an undeniable mark on this world. Thank you for being patient as I learned how to be a good mommy.

— To Mom and Dad. Thanks for loving me unconditionally and always wanting the best for me. I'm grateful that your marriage is still going strong after more than thirty-three years!

— To Grandma. Thanks for always keeping it real and being a listening ear. Your laughter is contagious!

— To my sister-in-law Leah. I can always depend on you for a hug or a listening ear. I love you and am so glad God blessed me with a sister!

— To my girlfriends—Corless, Denise, Tashawna, Kenya, Monee, Deatra, Joy, Shavonne, Kerri, Rhonda A., Rogelle, Angela, Remi, Sharlee, Melissa, Tracie, Christina, Sanja, Rhonda S., Wendy, Tiana, Mama Kimya, and Aunt Sue. You made me laugh. You let me cry. Your enduring friendship will never be denied!

— To Uncle Mark and Aunt Stephanie, Baba Charles and Mama Pam. I have never seen two couples have more fun—movie nights, date nights, and nonstop laughter! You have two of the healthiest marriages I've ever seen.

— To my sorority sisters and fellow authors, Jes'ka Washington and Christee Goode. Thanks for your encouragement and advice.

— To Pastor Booth and the Mt. Olivet Baptist Church family. Thanks for planting God's word in my heart at such a young age.

— To Rev. and Sister Lynch and the New Jerusalem Church family. Thanks for helping me develop spiritual maturity. Ms. Margaret, thanks for coordinating the women's retreats. Every summer, I look forward to relaxation and spiritual growth with my sisters.

— To my Warm Spirit family. Thank you for the positive and nurturing environment you provided and for allowing me to truly live up to my potential.

— To Remi, Kathy, Tracie, and Rhonda. Thank you for introducing me to life-changing self-development workshops with Landmark Education and DaniJohnson.com. Both of these seminars served as a turning point that led to Andre and I getting remarried. Thank you!

— To Debrena, Chandra, Uncle Mark, Pastor Lynch, and Andre. Thank you for graciously endorsing this book.

— Finally, to every reader. I pray that this personal memoir gives you hope, strength, and encouragement.

Introduction

November 18, 2003

The time is long overdue to write in my journal, to express my innermost thoughts in a deeply personal and private way. So much has happened since I last wrote five months ago. I attended my first national sorority convention. I went to Las Vegas for the first time. I even attended my first national convention for my new business, and was named a Top 10 recruiter across the company—wow!

Driving home from the convention, I felt extremely anxious, stopping several times because I felt sick to my stomach. When I got back in town, I went to Urgent Care. After stopping so many times to use the restroom, I was worried that maybe my grandmother's diabetes had skipped a generation and was now knocking at my door. Praise God, my body was in good shape, but when I walked into the house, my heart sank. The driveway was empty, and the house was dark, but in some strange way, I felt prepared for the next phase in my life. After all, Andre and I had agreed to separate from our marriage in May, just three months before my trip, and he had warned me that he would be moving out that weekend.

I had tried to forget about it during my trip, but the harsh reality slapped me in the face when I walked in the house. Nothing could have prepared me for what I experienced—the "wall of fame" where my husband and I had displayed our awards was half empty. The places where Andre's plaques, pictures, and honors once hung were left only with nails in a bare wall. The tears rushed out of my eyes as if freed from a dam. He moved out of our house, moved into his new home, and started a new life without me. He left. The excitement and exhilaration I had felt over the weekend quickly evaporated.

Although we had agreed to dissolve our marriage, I begged him not to send his teenage sister, who had lived with us for two years, back to Florida. I didn't want to cause more instability in her life, and more than anything, I didn't want to feel totally alone. So, my sister-in-law stayed with me and my daughter, but there was an unavoidable hole in my heart that couldn't be ignored. I cried, like I'm doing now, filled with sadness and grief. His sister hugged me and told me that it would be alright. I just had to "grip up and be strong."

The first couple weeks without Andre were tough. It was so difficult keeping everything together—both with our daughter and with his sister who continued to live with me for almost a year after he moved out. I had to get used to sleeping by myself, paying all the bills, and protecting the house, too. It didn't help matters when someone tried to break into my house. Luckily, I was out of town when it happened, but it scared me and reminded me that it was just me and God, just *me* and *God*. I think that's part of the plan. I've ignored God for so long that he wanted to get my attention, and he's gotten it alright.

This is a personal memoir of my journey toward forgiveness, wholeness, and restoration with my husband and with God. Based on a true story of marriage, divorce, and remarrying the same man, you'll learn the intimate details of how love was resurrected once I realized that I cheated on the one I needed to love the most—God—and how very dangerous it became to have mixed-up priorities. I pray that my story and the reflection questions in the book will help strengthen your relationship with God, yourself, and your current or future spouse.

–Kristin

Chapter 1

On a Mission to Find a Husband

What girl doesn't dream of being swept off of her feet and whisked away by her husband into a lifetime of bliss? At a young age, the rules of the game become clear. Part of your success as a girl (and woman), society tells us, includes being beautiful enough to attract a man. Having a boyfriend or husband earns you a stamp of approval; it's a sign that you've passed the test and are worth something. Regardless of your height, weight, color, or intellect, all little girls want a boyfriend, and some will stop at no end to get one.

In the emerging rap and hip-hop culture that I grew up in during the early '90s, it was popular to date a guy who was "hard," someone quick to fight if he had to. I grew up in the era when smoking "chronic" (weed) and "sippin' on gin and juice" were considered cool. In my teenage years, I remember declaring with my boyfriend, "I'll smoke weed 'til the day I die." Since being cool was now defined as doing illegal activities, it was nothing out of the ordinary for a girl or woman to date a drug dealer, gang member, or felon. I know—because I dated all three.

After graduating in the top 2 percent of my high school class in Columbus, Ohio, I went more than one thousand miles away to college at Florida A&M University, where I later graduated with both a bachelor's and master's degree in Business Administration. A model student, I served as student body president, leading more than one hundred staff members and volunteers and managing a quarter–million–dollar budget at the tender age of twenty-one. I was active in my sorority, where I founded an after-school rites of passage program that still exists today. I graduated summa cum laude with my MBA degree. Although my public life seemed almost perfect, privately, I felt a void. After all, during the first four years of college, I didn't go on a single date—that is, until I met Andre.

Toward the end of my term as student body president, I called a student government volunteer to inform him that the event he was coordinating had been cancelled because of budgetary constraints. Quickly striking up a conversation, he told me that he was new in town, a recently discharged Army veteran who was a twenty-two-year-old, first-semester freshman. He asked if I'd join him for dinner that Saturday night. "Sure," I replied, a bit taken aback at first that I'd been asked on a blind date. But then my surprise turned to excitement—I was going on a date! At the time, it didn't matter that I was more than halfway through my college career and he was a freshman. I soon came to find out that although we were the same age, we were at different stages in our lives.

Andre took me to dinner for our first date. The conversation was going well, until I found out that he didn't know—or care—that I was student body president! *"Who is this dude?"* I thought. Everyone who was *anyone* on campus seemed to know me, but I didn't hold it against him. After all, he was a freshman.

After dinner, neither of us wanted to go home, so we went to the movies. After the movie was over, we still didn't want to end the evening, so we went to the playground, where we spun around on the merry-go-round like children, laughing and giggling until 2 o'clock in the morning. Although we had fun that night, neither of us fell in love at first sight. But, over time, we began to know each other ... and like each other ... and love each other. Or so I thought.

A couple of years earlier, I'd written out a ten-year plan in my journal. At each age, I had milestones I wanted to reach and accomplishments I wanted to make. "Earn a graduate degree by the age of 23. Get married and start working at 24. Open a business by 29. Have my first child by 31." I had developed a will and determination that had allowed me to accomplish so many things already, so I had no doubt that those same qualities would help me transform my ten-year plan into reality. I was on track to graduate and get a job, so I became obsessed with finding a husband.

I knew the day was coming in our courtship when Andre would ask to officially start dating me. So I prepared. I thought about all the things I wanted in a man: good looks, a sense of humor, an adventurous spirit; someone who could take charge but also relax; and a good listener who would be protective of me and provide for our family. But, after more than six months of talking on the phone, I told Andre that he wasn't "marriage material." This broke his heart, and I realized later that it was an awful thing to say. Despite the litany of qualities that I laid out in my journal and the sacrifices Andre had made to take me out on expensive dates on his tight fast-food restaurant salary, I rejected Andre because of his thick military mustache and knee-high socks. Those qualities just weren't attractive to me!

I was so silly—I couldn't see then what I know now. He had all of the qualities I desired and more! My judgmental nature and superficial standards almost caused me to miss out on one of God's greatest gifts. I begged for his forgiveness the same night I made that awful comment, and while he forgave me, it didn't take away the sting of my hurtful and insensitive words. Although he claimed to forgive me, every so often Andre would tease me about not being "marriage material." It had been such an awful thing to say, especially when I later realized that he had all the qualities I ever dreamed of in a man.

Although Andre and I didn't have an immediate love connection, we liked each other as friends and continued to hang out after the "marriage material" comment. He was living on a tight income, and because he didn't have cable, he would come over to watch wrestling on my cable TV. I declared that he would have to watch it by himself, because I didn't like wrestling, but it didn't take long before I was drawn in by the wrestling storylines, and we started spending more and more time together. Now that the pressure to date was off, I began to open up and really get to know him. It felt like a wall had been torn down inside of me, and that created a more open space in which to communicate. Plus, because I had told him that I wasn't interested in dating him, he asked me to hook him up with one of my sorority sisters. I refused to do so before I at least gave him a shot. His interest in another woman was a sure-fire way to get me interested.

Andre talked often about his family—how much he loved his mom and his little sisters. He told me about their family trips and showed me video footage. I thought it was pretty weird, and I honestly couldn't understand how someone could talk about his family all the time. After all, I was an only child and didn't have family adventures like Andre had. But I came to appreciate his love for his family months later when I met and talked to them.

Andre and I continued to spend time together and went to countless WWE events, the movies, live jazz events, and for games of miniature golf. The more time I spent with him, the more I liked him, especially after he shaved his military mustache and folded down his socks.

Several months after courting, Andre said that he could see me "dressed in white," and something inside of me clicked. *"Could he be the one? Would my last name one day be Harper?"* I thought. From that moment forward, unbeknownst to him, our relationship was different. He became my whole world. I became dependent on him and the emotional support he provided. Instead of talking on the phone or hanging out with my friends, I spent all of my free time with Andre. We even worked together during the night shift at a residence facility for at-risk youth. We were together almost 24/7, and I was happily consumed. With his words, I became determined to marry him—no matter what the cost. Years later, I definitely paid a price.

Chapter 2

My Agenda Wasn't God's Plan

"I know what I'm doing. I have it all planned out—
plans to take care of you, not abandon you, plans to give
you the future you hope for."
(Jer. 29:11, *The Message*)

I graduated a year and a half after Andre and I began dating. A couple of months before my graduation, we broke up because he didn't want a long-distance relationship. However, he told me that one of the only reasons he would stay with me was if we got pregnant. Two months after starting a new corporate job, I was desperate and lonely. So I visited Andre during my alma mater's homecoming. He was a sophomore in college, and it was the five-year anniversary after I crossed into Delta Sigma Theta Sorority. I had paid to share a room with three of my sorority sisters, but I never stayed at the hotel. Instead, I stayed with Andre that weekend, and I took him up on his earlier offer. A few weeks later, I found out I was pregnant. Nine months later, our daughter was born. We were married a year after our daughter was born. The plan worked perfectly … for me.

Both of our families were excited when we told them they would soon have their first grandchild, but it didn't take long before we were encouraged—and pressured, in Andre's case—to get married. Since I wanted so desperately to get married, I also pressured Andre. After all, although my pregnancy came a few years ahead of schedule, the timing to get married was right on track with my ten-year plan.

During my pregnancy, Andre and I traveled to visit each other several times. One night while lying in bed, Andre asked for my hand in marriage, and although I said yes, I could sense the burden he felt. After all, he was only following through on a deal we had struck. I felt sick to my stomach and had a huge knot in my belly, and it wasn't the baby. I went to my sorority's party the next night, outwardly excited about the engagement, but inwardly torn because I knew my fiancé had asked for my hand in marriage out of obligation, not desire. I never took the time to put myself in Andre's shoes. Here, I had already graduated with *two* degrees and was gainfully employed, and all of a sudden, Andre now had the pressure not only to finish school, but also to take care of a new family. Because of his mother's debilitating illness, he already had custody of his teenage sister and was taking care of her. I never considered how difficult all this could be for someone who was only a sophomore in college.

After our daughter was born, I took several months off from work so Andre and I could be together with our new baby. We moved to Tallahassee, Florida, so Andre could enter his junior year in college at Florida A&M. I enjoyed the freedom of being at home and raising our daughter, but I knew it was temporary. In fact, I knew there was a strong possibility that it could be our last few days and weeks together as a family. I just felt it in my spirit. Although Andre loved being a father, he wasn't happy and felt like he'd been tricked into the situation. He told me—often.

People say that a bad man is better than no man at all, but I didn't want to live in house where someone felt forced to be there. You can't have love under force. Although I didn't regret our daughter for one second, I definitely regretted the decisions that led to becoming parents. Just before I moved back to Ohio to return to work after an extended maternity leave, I wrote a poem that expressed my heart's anguish. For once, I stopped being superficial and instead looked at the situation with emotional honesty. I was preparing for the worst and hoping for the best.

I'm Three Days Away from Being a Single Parent

I'm three days away from being a single parent
Who ever thought it would turn out this way?
What ever happened to dreams of *my* Huxtable
family?
It's starting to appear that dreams are far, far
away.
It's ironic because my mom didn't raise me like
this.

There were just certain things we didn't do—
Having babies out of wedlock, getting strung
    out on drugs—
That was for other people, but not for *us* to do…
Ain't it funny how those little phrases Mama
    used to say
Will always come back to haunt you?
They're really wise words, not a haunt at all,
And they force you to analyze truth.
"Don't get pregnant to keep no man!"
I heard her say right before he came inside.
But I did it, Mama, and it backfired like a
    mutha
And I just wanna run and go hide.
I'd never tell you 'cause I feel so much shame;
I consciously made a mistake'
Now a daughter, a ring, and thirteen months
    later
I feel like my soul's gonna break.
Trying to make it work when the spark is long
    gone
Gets real old, and I know it won't last.
This engagement's a joke, pressure shoved down
    our throats.
I just wish this would stay in the past.
But a part of it can't 'cause my future is filled
With my daughter, and it seems so apparent.
Time to get it together, somebody needs me bet-
    ter—
I'm three days away from being a single parent.

                                              —Kristin

Do you ever hear that little voice inside your head? Do you ever get that certain feeling in your gut? Whether you acknowledge or ignore them, they're there, and they will eventually get your attention—they're the Holy Spirit. After our engagement and even through the wedding ceremony, I heard that voice and felt that feeling several times, but I ignored it. The spirit told me to stop faking like everything was alright. They reminded me that Andre was unhappy, and so was I.

More than once, we tried to call off the engagement. On the eve of my bridal shower, I told my mother that we were calling off the wedding. Wanting no part of it, she refused to acknowledge, much less accept, our decision. On another occasion, Andre wanted to call off the engagement, but I lamented and wailed about how I would be embarrassed among my friends if we called it quits. After all, we'd invested too many years together to end up with nothing! That was bad thinking rooted in selfishness. In reality, we had only been together for two years, which wasn't very long at all.

The Holy Spirit is a comforter, but I could also feel the Spirit wrestling with my mind and heart. Throughout the engagement, I knew, without a shadow of a doubt, that Andre and I shouldn't get married, but I ignored God's voice and opted for my selfish plans instead because I had an image to uphold. If we had obtained marriage counseling, I'm almost certain that I would have had the courage to say no to the marriage. I had manipulated Andre into getting married, and a part of me was scarily okay with that, but there was no *way* I would have manipulated, negotiated with, or lied to God. God was the ultimate authority, and I couldn't pull any fast ones over on him. So instead of facing the truth, I avoided God (and marriage counseling) so I wouldn't have to make that tough decision to call off the wedding and stick to the decision, but I failed to recognize that my actions had already made the decision for me.

Despite our indecisiveness, Andre told me that he'd honor his word and marry me, but he would probably be unhappy in the marriage. He even said that we would probably divorce one day. He was honest with me, and it seems like, after hearing his words, I would have looked at the situation objectively and made a decision to leave—but I stayed. I was just happy that someone loved me enough to *ask* for my hand in marriage. I had no idea that Andre's prophetic words would eventually come to pass.

Andre moved to Ohio, and we had a beautiful wedding ceremony and reception. We had twelve people in our bridal party, and more than three hundred friends and family members traveled across the country to be with us. I custom designed the ceremony with beautiful songs and memorable rituals. One such ritual was the ceremony of the bitter and sweet. In this African tradition, we tasted different elements to represent the various stages we would experience in our marriage. First there was lemon to represent the sour moments. Then we tasted cayenne pepper for those hot, spicy, sensual times. We also tasted vinegar for the bitter times, and finally honey for the sweet. If this ceremony were any indication of what the future might hold, we were in store for some rough times.

At the altar, when it came time to say the vows, Andre paused for what seemed to me like a lifetime before saying, "I do." Unsure of what was on his mind, I was just relieved that he got through the vows. *"Thank God he got through the vows. I hope no one else noticed his hesitation. What if people knew that we made a deal?"* I thought. But the deal was done, and we were now husband and wife. My plan had worked to a tee!

Our honeymoon was far from "honeyed"—it felt more bitter than sweet, and I knew it couldn't be a good start for a marriage. Even though Andre tried to hide his feelings, I couldn't help but see how unhappy he was. In all of these instances, I ignored the voice inside and dismissed my true feelings, justifying each circumstance in order to feel like I had made a smart decision and was doing the right thing.

Immediately after returning from our honeymoon, I started a home-based business. I was excited about the opportunity to enhance people's lives while making money. The business took over everything. After working a full-time job each day, I came home, only to work for two to three more hours in my business, leaving absolutely no time for my husband or daughter. Unconsciously, my business became my top priority, which resulted in me ignoring, and by default *deprioritizing*, my family.

I was so focused on my business that I never noticed that Andre was raising our daughter, cleaning the house, cooking for the family virtually by himself. I was so focused on my business that I couldn't see a storm brewing in my own house. Later, it not only rained, it poured.

There was one situation I couldn't ignore. On the eve of my birthday, just five months after getting married, I decided to go out with friends to see a play. It seemed reasonable that I would celebrate on Friday with friends, and Saturday—my actual birth date—with my husband. But I made plans with my friends with no consideration for Andre. I figured that he could take care of the baby while I went out, and we would celebrate together on Saturday. However, when I got home from the play, the house was eerily dark and silent. Andre was sitting alone in the living room, wide awake but with the lights completely off. The look on his face told the whole story. That night, I realized his sadness and misery in our marriage and recognized my lack of regard for him. Andre told me that he had become sad and depressed.

That night I wrote in my journal:

February 2004

It's only been five months since we got married, and I often wonder if we will last five years. After all, how long can I stay in a relationship that I know was wrong from the beginning? It's my birthday weekend, and I'm crying my eyes out. I thought I could go to a play tonight with my friends and to a concert with Andre tomorrow on the actual day of my birthday. It didn't occur to me until I walked in the door earlier this evening that I chose my friends over him. But I didn't do it consciously. Am I selfish? Maybe. Do I have too much to do on my plate? I think so. I have a crumbling marriage, a depressed husband, and the pride of a lion. That's a bad combination.

That night, things changed. My spirit was awakened, and I became more in tune than ever to Andre's needs and feelings. Over the next couple of months, I tried everything I could to be a better wife. I spent more time with Andre and less time on the computer and telephone. I did more chores instead of letting him carry the load by himself. I spent more time playing with our daughter and less time working. But it was too little, too late. Andre was determined that our marriage was irreconcilable, and I decided that I would no longer be the cause of his sadness. I refused to let my hands be stained with the guilt of doing anything possible to keep him in this marriage when he was clearly unhappy. Regrettably, I had to let him go.

May 11, 2004

Today is May 11th, 2004, nearly three months since my "aha" moment, and my husband is leaving. We mutually agreed that we need to separate. He's meeting a Realtor tomorrow to place an offer on a house. He's sending his sister back home to live with other family members. He's not abandoning me or our daughter, nor is he running away from responsibility. He's running away from death. He told me that he's been dying inside over the past several months, and he can't take it anymore. He told me that it's time to put himself first and everyone else second.

I'm hurt. I'm weeping. My biggest fear has come to fruition. In fact, just a few weeks ago, I asked Andre if we could go see his family for Easter. In the back of my mind, I knew we wouldn't be together by Thanksgiving. Sure enough, it's coming true.

What have I learned? You can't force anyone to love you, especially if the magic is gone. Putting other people's needs before your own—and ignoring your needs in the process—is not sustainable. If people aren't ready, let them be. If they ask for time, and you don't give it, don't be fooled … they'll get it sooner or later. Never have a baby to keep a man.

That's enough. Enough lessons, enough to keep the tears from overflowing while Andre walks out the door.

Lord, please give me strength to handle this breakup. Please help me to keep my head held high and my mind focused on you. Please help me to be the best mother I can be. Please help me to count my blessings and to name them one by one. Lord, please keep our friendship intact if it is your will. More than anything, I'm not going to ask that we get back together, but please, just let your will be done, and let me accept whatever it is that you have for my life.

- Krissy

We couldn't lie anymore. Our marriage wasn't working. Nine months after we said, "I do," Andre moved out, and less than two years after getting married, we were legally divorced. Sad, lonely, hurt, and embarrassed by what I considered to be my first failure in life, I turned to the one I'd been ignoring for so long. I ran into the arms of God.

Kristin R. Harper

Reflection Questions

1. Write about a time when you chose your agenda over God's plan.

_____

_____

_____

_____

_____

2. Write about a time when you ignored the Holy Spirit. What was the consequence?

_____

_____

_____

_____

_____

3. When the does Holy Spirit speak to you? How can you discern the voice of the Holy Spirit from your own will?

_____

_____

_____

_____

_____

Chapter 3

Pruning

*"The fun and games are over. Get serious, really serious.
Get down on your knees before the Master; it's the only
way you'll get on your feet."*
(James 4:9–10, *The Message*)

The first weekend in August, Andre moved out.
This was also the weekend of my business convention. I had decided before my drive from our home in Cincinnati to Chicago that I would fast from secular music; I knew that hearing love songs on the radio would only worsen the pain. So during the five-hour drive to and from the conference—and for seven months afterwards—I listened only to gospel music. It uplifted my soul and provided me hope. It reminded me of the spiritual foundation that my parents and church community had laid for me years before.

The energy of the convention and the gospel music I'd listened to kept my spirit lifted throughout the weekend. I had received a national award for my results over the past year, and it felt like I was on top of the world. But nothing would have prepared me for the feelings of emptiness and devastation I experienced after returning home. Where our awards, medals, and trophies once stood was now a half-empty wall. It was official: Our marriage was dying, and I was alone.

I could have let my marriage die and gone on with my life. I could have chosen to start fresh in a new relationship with a new man so I could forget about Andre. However, I chose to prune the dead branches of our relationship so I could heal naturally over time. Pruning is a very interesting process. According to dictionary.com, pruning is "cutting off or removing dead or living parts or branches, of a plant, for example, to improve shape or growth." When the branches of a tree die, they're cut back and sometimes cut off completely. During the pruning process, even the healthy branches can be cut back. At first glance, one would think that growing new branches would take much longer than the original growth period, but the opposite is true. The branches grow back stronger, more quickly, and more beautiful than before.

In Romans 11, Paul talks about two olive trees. One was a wild, untamed olive tree, and the other was a strong olive tree with plenty of fruit. Instead of letting the wild branches go untamed and unconnected to their roots, a few dead branches were cut from the wild olive tree and grafted them into the branches of the strong olive tree. As the branches grew together, the branches from the wild olive tree adopted the roots and robustness of the strong olive tree; after all, the branches are only as strong as their roots, and the roots are only as strong as the seed.

This story illustrates a few key lessons:

1. **Death is an inevitable, natural, and necessary process.** During the course of our existence, some things in our lives will die. This could be a hope, a dream, or an unfulfilled desire; a relationship, a friendship, or a marriage. But one thing in life is certainly inevitable—death. Death, however, does not equate to destruction; in fact, death makes room for something new to be born, be it confidence, faith, or character. This is only possible when we are connected to our "roots," that is, a strong value system.

2. **You can always tap into another source of strength.** Among the trees were both good fruit and bad fruit. Had the branches of the wild tree not been removed and given new life in the strong, healthy tree, they would have remained wild and uncontrollable. In the same way, there is always someone or something stronger than you that you can rely upon for strength— whether it's God, a role model, or someone's testimony—and sometimes you just have to encourage yourself.

3. **With death, there is opportunity for life.** So many times we are sad, lonely, and withdrawn when death occurs, but one of the most important processes in life is allowing yourself

to grieve. Although death and loss can leave a gaping hole, the gap shouldn't be left empty forever. The dead branches were intermingled with healthy, I understand your thoughts; I've added more context on the dead branches above (confirmed in the passage as well), and would like to keep the word dead 1) because it's referred to as "deadwood" in The Message and 2) it demonstrates God's ability to resurrect even what's dead.fruitful branches whose roots were strong and enduring, and this grafting process resurrected a once-dead branch.

4. **Your branches are only as strong as your roots and the seed that has been planted.** Often people tell stories about one good apple spoiling the bunch. This story has a different twist: integrating one weak branch into a strong tree with healthy roots transformed the weak branch, and the previously weak branch will now yield healthy fruit instead of rotten fruit. If you don't like the fruit that's growing on your tree, trace the fruit back to the root and then to the seed that was planted.

There were so many dead branches on my "tree" before, during, and after my marriage—selfishness, arrogance, and pride. Although my parents had planted seeds of confidence, faith, risk-taking, and adventure years before, I had accomplished so many things throughout my twenty-five years of life that I'd become somewhat arrogant. I'd graduated with honors from college, traveled the world, and started five profitable businesses. Yet in relationships, seeds of being "too fat," "too smart," and "too plain" caused me to feel like a failure, resulting in branches of low self-esteem and lack of confidence. The embarrassment I tried to avoid by breaking up during the engagement came back to haunt me.

I retreated from the world—my mood became somber, and my once-contagious optimism seemed to disappear. I slowly told my closest friends the news of our separation, but I kept my tears private. Even my co-workers had no idea of the inner turmoil I experienced. I kept a poker face by day and the tears of a clown by night. That Christmas, I went to a holiday party and was reminded several times that Andre was really gone.

December 10, 2004

I get tired of people asking where my husband is. I can only avoid answering their questions for so long, or acting like I don't hear people. I'm tired of being sad and depressed. My heart is heavy, but I'm hesitant to share my pain. I'm surrounded by people, but I feel all alone. I've never been so pessimistic—I'm trying to get back to my optimistic self.

Tonight was the holiday party with my African American affinity group from work—I took my daughter and sister-in-law. When I saw my friend's husband, he asked where Andre was, but I pretended not to hear. Then my daughter vomited in three different places around the house. I was on my hands and knees, holding my daughter in one hand, and wiping vomit off the leather couch and new cream-colored carpet when my friend's husband asked again, "Is your husband here?" "No," I replied curtly, and my heart got heavy. My eyes starting welling up with tears, and I knew that I needed to leave before my tears escaped. My sister-in-law was an absolute angel and helped to clean up the mess with two of my co-workers. Thank God for all of the people who helped, but despite all of them, I still felt all alone. Alone.

Even now, I'm crying, and my two-and-a-half-year-old daughter is telling me, "It's okay, Mommy's crying, but it's okay." All the while, she's rubbing my arm and holding me close. What a sweet baby.

I'm writing in a workbook, and one of the exercises was to write down your beliefs about men, women, money, work, and God. What was most revealing is that my belief about women, men, and work were all negative. I had a few positive beliefs about women, but the majority of my beliefs were negative. And I don't like it. So, I'm changing my beliefs.

Change your beliefs, change your thoughts, change your actions, change your life. This is only the beginning. The healing process begins *today*.

~ *Kristin*

My plan of being a wife and mother had been fulfilled, but my hopes for happiness were fading. During my reflections on our failed marriage, I realized that I was more concerned with the ceremony than the matrimony. You see, I had dreamed of being a wife and mother, and I was so happy that someone loved me enough to marry me. I wondered how many people would come to see me on my big day. I dreamed of the wedding ceremony—how beautiful it would be, how princess-like I would look. Maybe I was even more in love with the *idea* of being loved than actually loving my husband. Getting married had always been a dream, though; it meant life was complete! But I realized that my desire to get married was rooted in self-centeredness, which led to being inflexible. It was my way or the highway, and Andre chose the highway.

Like it or not, I was a single mom who wanted to spend my life with my husband, and although Andre loved me, the harsh reality was that he didn't want to be with me. Andre often told me that he didn't think I deserved him. Although I felt like this was an arrogant statement at the time, I started to understand the truth behind his words. I didn't reciprocate the type of love he demonstrated toward me, and I understood why he got fed up. The pride I once had was now replaced with humility, because I realized that I wasn't invincible, nor was I immune from being hurt. Our impending divorce was for real.

I also realized for the first time that I wasn't perfect. I know that sounds silly, but I'd been pretty smart all my life. I'd generally made good choices, and becoming another divorce statistic was a serious blow to my self-esteem and to the superwoman image I had successfully created. I started to analyze the choices I'd made, and honestly, they weren't always very wise. I realized that I'd played an undeniable role in the demise of our marriage, in fact, a much more detrimental role than I'd realized before.

So, for the first time, I pulled off my mask. I just couldn't stand the sense of uneasiness in my spirit, and I was tired of acting like everything was fine— it *wasn't.* For too long, I had resisted looking at my life with emotional honesty, but this time I let it all out and withheld judgment. I didn't justify what I felt to try to make me feel like what I'd done was right. I just told our story without embellishments. I journaled and journaled and journaled. I wrote until my fingers were numb, and what I uncovered was far from pretty: selfishness, low self-esteem, and lack of self-confidence.

After I wrote the story of our lives, I read the story as if I were reading about a friend. It's funny how obvious the answer is when it's someone else's life—it just doesn't seem as easy to analyze your own situation. But through this exercise, I realized that I loved what I had accomplished in life but didn't love myself for who I *was*—someone who had become insecure, controlling, and desperate. No wonder why our marriage failed. How could I love someone else when I didn't even love myself?

Reflection Questions

1. What type of "fruit" are you producing on your tree?

_____

_____

_____

_____

2. The fruit can be traced back to the roots, and the roots to the seeds. What type of seeds were planted, when, and by whom?

_____

_____

_____

_____

_____

3. What branches in your life need to be pruned, if any? What possibilities could result from pruning these branches?

_____

_____

_____

_____

_____

4. What new seeds would you like to plant in your tree of life? What type of fruit do you want to produce as a result of these new seeds that will take root?

_____

_____

_____

_____

_____

Chapter 4

The Desires of My Heart

Mother's Day 2005

It's Mother's Day, and I just came home from the movies. I'm thinking about what I desire in a companion. Just yesterday, I had a conversation with a friend during which I told her about the situation with my dying marriage. She began to tell me how she dated her husband more months than they were married, and to my surprise, she is now in her second marriage.

She talked about the things she had requested from God—the desires she had of her next husband. She divorced when her daughter was one year old and met her current husband when her daughter was five. She talked about her desire for a seamless family and a companion who would love her daughter as his own. I knew her husband, and by his interactions with their daughter, and I would have never guessed that he wasn't her biological father. That day, she instilled hope in me and provided reassurance that God could make it better the second time around.

And ever since yesterday, I've been thinking about my desires. I've been trying to talk to God. I really can't figure out much more that I want out of anybody else that I didn't have in Andre. I guess more than anything, I want more out of *myself.* I expect more *from* myself. That's why I've been struggling in the conversation with God.

On my third Mother's Day, I fixed my mind not to expect anything from Andre. After all, he's hates holidays and seems to forget them anyway. I wanted to keep my expectations low so I wouldn't be disappointed. But no sooner than I came home did I see a dozen roses with a card from Andre.

The tears just pour out—they've been waiting to be released for a while now. And I cry and cry and cry out of joy because he remembered, out of thankfulness because he loves me, but also out of sadness because there aren't many more desires I have of a companion that Andre doesn't possess. I was the one who didn't demonstrate those qualities, not him. I cry because I messed up. I drove Andre away because of pressure and selfishness. And now, I'm going to the movies alone on Saturday nights while he's going to black-tie affairs—maybe by himself and maybe with someone else, but it's not me, and it reminds me even more how I messed up!

It's hard to admit how selfish I've been, how much hurt I've caused him, and how guilty I feel for the pain and suffering I've caused. And I know that I loved Andre selfishly, while he loved me sacrificially and without condition. It's clear that I pale in comparison to the unselfish love Andre demonstrates, even during our separation.

All I want is a second chance, a chance to make things right and show that I've learned and I know better and I'll do better. But it's too late with Andre. The divorce papers are filed, and we're waiting on a court date. Are lessons really that valuable if you can't practice what you've learned?

Good night, Happy Mother's Day to me. I'm crying my selfish self to sleep.

~ KRH

As I continued to uncover the hidden truths of my life, I made a sad discovery. Andre was *everything* to me—I idolized him. With him, I felt whole and complete, and when he left, I felt empty. In fact, when I looked honestly at my priorities, they looked like this:

1. Work/my business

2. Andre

3. Our daughter

4. God

5. Family and friends

6. Community

And when I was really honest with myself, the foundation of my priorities was all about *me: my* wants, *my* plans, *my* desires, and *my* agendas. I was selfish and manipulative, and I'm convinced that my selfishness contributed to the destruction of our marriage. Because it was all about me, I didn't have the capacity to love anyone else. This selfishness showed up in every area of my life. I typically called family and friends only when I needed something. In my business, I showed concern for my customers and business partners when I needed their sales, time, or effort. I worked in the community to make myself look good. The glory of my life was not for God; it was for me.

It was starting to make sense. The decision to go to the play on my birthday, and assuming that Andre would watch our daughter, was selfish. Being too embarrassed among friends to do what we thought was best for our relationship and call off the wedding was inherently self-centered. Never mind how he felt—*I* didn't want to be embarrassed. I didn't like the fruit on any of my branches, and I certainly didn't like the roots from which it stemmed—insecurity, control, and manipulation.

There is a passage of scripture that came back to my remembrance—"nothing shall separate me from the love of God that is in Christ Jesus our Lord" (Rom. 8:39, NIV). I realized that God was no longer a top priority in my life. I ignored that still, small voice telling me, "No, it's not right for you to get married now." In fact, I didn't even pray for discernment or guidance in deciding whether to get married, a decision that changed my life forever. I didn't heed the teaching I'd learned in Sunday school years earlier: "Trust in the Lord with all thine heart, and lean not unto your own understanding. In all thy ways, acknowledge Him, and He shall direct your path" (Prov. 3:5-6). I consulted God when I needed help, or rather, when I *wanted* his help. There was never a point when I trusted him with *all* of my heart, acknowledged *his* will for my life, or let *his* guidance overpower my bull-headed rationale.

Although God tells us to consult him in every decision we make, he still gives us free will and allows us to make our own choices. However, he won't let his sheep go astray for too long. The shepherd knows his sheep, and even if ninety-nine of his one hundred are safe, he won't quit until the one comes back home (Luke 15:1–7). By getting married outside of his will, I went astray, and God needed to get my attention to gently guide me back home.

This may surprise you, but getting divorced was one of the best things that ever happened in my life. Although the marriage wasn't under God's direction, I believe everything that happened was ordained by God and part of the plan he had for my life. Had we not divorced, I wouldn't have restored God back to his rightful place as the head of my life. I may have not repented and turned from my "wicked ways" of selfishness, control, and manipulation (2 Chron. 7:14). Furthermore,

I wouldn't have been able to tell the story of God's redemptive love and modern-day resurrection power.

For the first time, I admitted my shortcomings to my ex-husband and humbly asked for forgiveness. We were able to close the chapter on issues that had been lingering for years and years. God tore down the high places in my life that had separated me from his love, even taking away the person I loved the most. It taught me that one (person) with God is a majority. Now I truly know that "All things work together for the good of those who love the Lord and are called according to His purpose" (Rom 8:28).

"If you remain in me and my words remain in you, ask whatever you wish, and it will be given you" (John 15:7). Because God allows us to ask for whatever we want, that's exactly what I did.

May 2005

I've learned from others that it's okay to ask God for what you want—to proclaim your desires and to make them known. So, here goes. These are my desires.

- I desire to love myself so much that I take care of myself. That means right eating, right movement (exercise), right detoxification, and right rest.

- I desire that my daughter love God and obey his word. I desire that she hide the word in her heart so she won't sin against God.

- I desire that working in my passions will

provide a substantial income, and continuing to be humble and thankful to God.

- I desire that God will provide a helpmate, soul mate, friend, confidante, and lover with whom I can spend my life. I pray for a man who loves God, serves God, obeys God, and makes God first in his life.

- I pray that I don't have to go to a club to find a man! Enough said.

- I desire a man who will love my daughter like his own, welcome the blended family, and simply adore me, flaws and all.

- I pray for someone whom I don't have to "save" as a hero, someone who can take us both to higher heights, instead of me having to over-compensate for his lacking.

- I desire healing—a whole heart, mended and ready to love again. I desire the spirit of unselfish giving and true sacrifice. I desire wholeness like I've never known before.

More than anything, I desire peace and God's will to be done. I want to—no I *do*—surrender all to you, God. My life, my will, my heart, my mind. No more will peace be forfeited, no more needless pains will be borne. I will take everything to God in prayer.

These are my desires, but let your will be done, God.

With love,

~ Krissy

Putting God first meant that my selfish intentions had to die. It meant that my very life was intended to serve other and not just to be served. It meant that I was here to love others and not just to be loved. The separation and eventual divorce was a humbling experience; for the first time in my life, I felt like I had failed. Here, I had been admired, respected, and honored by so many college classmates, professors, and others, but privately, I felt like a total failure. On the outside, I was almost a saint, but the truth was that I was a sinner. I had been blind to the impact that my selfishness had on others, especially my family, and I earnestly and honestly confessed for having been so wicked.

One thing I love about God is that, unlike people, he forgives *and* forgets. Here I was feeling guilty about all of my blunders and mistakes, but his voice was always gentle and comforting. In his presence, the guilt and shame of the past disappeared, and I felt safe, which transformed my feeling of pain into joy. You would not believe the amount of peace I felt letting go of selfish intentions, and letting God be my guide.

Reflection Questions

1. List your priorities, in order. Be honest with yourself.

1. _____

2. _____

3. _____

4. _____

5. _____

6. _____

7. _____

2. Is anything or anyone separating you from the love of God? How does this affect you and your relationships?

3. How can you demonstrate that God is the first priority in your life?

Kristin R. Harper

4. What are the desires of your heart?

_____

_____

_____

_____

_____

Chapter 5

My New Sugar Daddy

For the first time in my life, I was excited about getting to know God. The more I learned, the more fascinated I became. I had purchased a new Bible called *The Message*, which is written in contemporary, easy-to-understand language. Reading *The Message*, I found the Bible to be "juicy"—I didn't have to watch soap operas or other TV dramas, because the Bible was filled with so much drama itself! I'd gone through periods before when I'd recommit myself to God and do all the right things for a while—prayer, meditation, Bible study, and living my life for God's glory—before slipping back into my old habits of doing whatever I wanted to do with no thought of who I was doing it for. In most cases, I was trying to look good and impress people with my intellect, skills, and abilities for my own glory, but this time was different—God was no longer an option; this time, he was a necessity.

I didn't really know how to get to know God again, but I figured that it had to be similar to dating. Let's look at the dating process. First, you spend time getting to know the other person's likes and dislikes, characteristics and personality, dreams and desires. You test each other to see how the other will respond. If the person's reliable, you start to slowly reveal more personal and confidential information to build confidence and evaluate how discreet he or she can be. As you get to know and like each other better, you spend more and more time together, and you may even tell friends and family about this special person.

If all goes well, your conversations will become more serious. You'll start to talk about the future and your intentions together. Eventually comes the ultimate question of commitment—"Will you marry me?" Marriage takes a couple to the deepest levels of intimacy—physically, spiritually, and emotionally—and you spend your life together, following through with the pledges you made to each other.

During this time, I led a church workshop at our women's retreat on communing with God, and I gave an illustration of getting to know God using the dating process. The first date went like this:

> **God:** Hey, how are you? I saw you from afar the other day, and I just wanted to get to know you better.

> **Woman:** Yeah, well, you seem really interesting to me too. I appreciate you asking me out. I'm looking forward to getting to know you.

God: Yeah, me too. So tell me about yourself.

Woman: Well, I'm twenty-seven years old. I was born in Columbus and graduated from Florida A&M University. I work in marketing. I own my own home, my own car, I have an investment portfolio, and I even have my own business. What about you?

God: About me … I'm patient, I'm just, gracious, slow to anger, plenteous in mercy. I take care of those who love me … I protect my people. See, for me, it's not about the outward appearance. It's not about where you went to school or how many possessions you have. Man looks at the outward appearance, but I look at the heart.

Woman: Wow. I've never met a man who valued my inner self more than my outer appearance. That's pretty impressive.

God: You'll soon find that there's no one like me in all the earth. So tell me about your last relationship.

Woman: My last relationship ended because my boyfriend, at the time, didn't want to commit to me. He wasn't ready for a long-term relationship, and I wasn't willing to wait. I felt like

I'd been dumped and rejected. It was a hurtful breakup, and I'm still healing from it. I don't want to be in that situation again, so now I'm just having fun dating.

God: Well, one thing you should know about me: I will never leave you nor forsake you. You won't find me to be a fair-weather friend. I'll stick by you in the good times and the bad, closer than a brother.

Woman: I had a funny situation with the last guy I met. He was a doctor. He graduated from an Ivy League school; he had his own place and drove a Benz. He seemed to have everything going for him, and he was fine! He complimented me on my appearance, which was flattering, but at the end of the dinner, he wanted to take it further than I was willing to go—on the first date!

God: Everything that looks good to you isn't always good for you. You won't find that type of situation with me. Dinners are nice, but here's how I want us to get to know each other better. First of all, we have to identify our likes and dislikes. What are your desires? What do you despise? For example, I like being loved, but I hate being second priority. We also need to understand each other's character—what is it about you that makes you you? How would other people describe you? People call me wonderful, counselor, the mighty God, the everlasting father, the Prince of Peace, a bridge over troubled water, a rock in a weary land, bread when they're hungry, water when they're thirsty. What is your character, and how would people describe you?

Next, what are your dreams and desires? I desire praise—in fact, I demand it. I want people like you to love me, and I need to be first in your life. I want you to be saved so you can live forever with me, but when people turn their backs on me, it breaks my heart.

There's so much more that I want to know about you, but let me suggest some ways we can work through this. First, it's important that we have a private relationship. I'll meet your friends and your family and other people who are significant to you, and it's okay to share the joy that we bring into each other's lives. But it's not all about what they think of me or what they perceive of our relationship—it's about me and you. It's our one-to-one relationship that's most important.

Second, communication will make or break our relationship. Sometimes that means talking to one another and listening to one another without distractions. It means being honest with our desires and with our pain. There are times when we'll be together but not say a word; we'll just be present with each other through silence, meditation, communion, feeling, sensing, and being. Can you do that?

Woman: Well, that sounds good, but this is a little new to me. After we start talking more, I'll probably begin to recognize and discern your voice. The key is for me to stop talking all the time and to instead be 100 percent in tune with you.

God: That's exactly right. Distractions are many—TV, music, work, to-do lists, even people—and there are times when, for the sake of our relationship, we'll need to ignore outside distractions and only be with each other. That will help us to deepen our connection one to another. This might sound strange, but sometimes my messages won't be spoken by me. Sometimes another person may give you a message, or things just kind of fall into place, unbeknownst to you. Or a natural event could occur to give you a clue to the message I'm sending. You must know me and trust me to decipher the clues along the journey. If you ask, the Holy Spirit will help you figure out what my will is for you.

Third, I know you enjoy spending time with your friends, but in order for us to build a solid relationship, we need to spend as much time together as you do with your friends, and probably more. I want your life to be transformed by our relationship. Put my word up around you. Remind yourself of how good I am, and do it often! Let your praise for me continually be on your lips because I will take care of you, regardless of what happens. You can rest assured that if you love me, everything—regardless of whether you think it's good or bad for you—everything in your life will work out for your good.

Finally, if you *really* want to get to know me, I've written a guide called the Bible. There are several different versions to choose from, so you can find one suited toward your preference. There are many ways to learn about my character through the Bible. There are sermons, parables, and real-life stories; you can go to Bible study, Sunday school, or vacation Bible school; you can even study on your own by reading or listening to books on tape. Take your pick—but only do this if you really want to get to know me. Don't worry—I already know all about you. Before I formed you, I knew you. And even though I already know everything about you— your thoughts, feelings, beliefs, dreams, desires, likes, and dislikes—I will always listen to your every cry.

Woman: Wow, I can't wait to get to know you. I can feel it—none of my ex-boyfriends could even compare to the relationship I'm about to have with you! So when will we talk again?

God: I'm always available—will you take the time to be available for me? You can call me day or night, and we should talk often. At a minimum, though, please talk to me when you wake up and before you go to sleep.

Woman: Sounds great. I'll talk to you tonight.

Getting to know God is much like the dating process. I started spending time with God through prayer, meditation, praise, worship, and studying after I took an inventory of how I spent my time and who I was living for, because I realized that the way I spent my time didn't align to my new priority of God being number one in my life. Spending time with God almost became addicting—the more I learned, the more I wanted to learn. I began attending Bible study to learn more about God—his likes, dislikes, promises, and the stories on how he worked in other people's lives. With every story, I gained more hope. I became more and more conscious of my thoughts, actions, and behaviors, and I repented for making myself the center of attention throughout my life. I started practicing agape love and treating others how I wanted to be treated. I wanted God's spirit to shine through me for his glory.

I started trusting him with my finances, what I believe is the ultimate measure of faith. Although I had always tithed, I started tithing based on my gross income rather than on my net income. I was really putting God first, even with my money, and I have *never* wanted for anything. In fact, I have been blessed beyond what I could have ever imagined.

What's so funny is that as I drew closer to God I had no desire to date any men—I was too occupied with getting my heart right; plus, there was absolutely nothing I could have offered. I was still a work under construction. But I did become more intimate with God through the "dating" process, and I learned a few of the things God likes and dislikes of us:

God likes for us to ...

- **Love him:** "Love the Lord your God with all of your heart and with all your soul and with all your strength." (Deut. 6:5)

- **Trust him:** "Trust in the Lord with all thine heart and lean not to thine own understanding. In all thy ways, acknowledge Him and He shall direct thy path." (Prov. 3:5–6)

- **Take comfort in him:** "Come unto me, all ye that labour and are heavy laden, and I will give you rest." (Matt. 11:28)

- **Pursue him:** "… he that cometh to God must believe that he is, and that he is a rewarder of them that diligently seek him." (Heb. 11:6)

- **Wait on him:** "But they that wait upon the Lord shall renew their strength; they shall mount up with wings as eagles; they shall run, and not be weary; and they shall walk, and not faint." (Isa. 40:31)

— **Let him be our guide:** "And I will bring the blind by a way that they knew not; I will lead them in the paths that they have not known: I will make darkness light before them, and crooked things straight. These things will I do unto them, and not forsake them." (Isa. 42:16)

— **Confess our sins to him:** "If we confess our sins, he is faithful and just to forgive us our sins, and to cleanse us from all unrighteousness." (1 John 1:9)

— **Humble ourselves before him:** "And whosoever shall exalt himself shall be abased; and he that shall humble himself shall be exalted." (Matt. 23:12)

— **Be glad in him:** "But let the righteous be glad; let them rejoice before God: yea, let them exceedingly rejoice." (Ps. 68:3)

God dislikes …

— **Being second priority:** "Thou shall have no other gods before me." (Exod. 20:3)

— **Fearfulness:** "And he saith unto them, 'Why are ye so fearful? How is it that ye have no faith?'" (Mark 4:40)

— **Wickedness:** "The Lord preserveth all them that love him: but all the wicked will he destroy." (Ps. 145:20)

- **Pride, lying, murder, conspiracy, eagerness to do wrong, being a troublemaker, and adultery:** "Here are six things God hates, and one more that he loathes with a passion: eyes that are arrogant, a tongue that lies, hands that murder the innocent, a heart that hatches evil plots, feet that race down a wicked track, a mouth that lies under oath, a troublemaker in the family. For a prostitute will bring you to poverty, but sleeping with another man's wife will cost you your life." (Prov. 6:6-19, 26, *The Message* and *New Living Translation*)

The more I learned about God's character, the more I admired Andre. I had been in church all my life—I could count on two hands how many Sundays I'd missed a worship service. I could quote scripture, I knew dozens of hymns by heart, I'd sung in the choir, and I'd even served as a church musician since I was a teenager. Surely, I had been a good Christian, right? Wrong. I had been raised believing that my works would get me into heaven. So the barometer by which I measured my Christian faith was religious norms and traditions. However, religion was manmade, and God was more concerned with my walk than my work.

Likewise, Andre had been raised in the church. His great-great-grandmother founded a holiness church that expanded across the country. He, too, went to church, but he wasn't as worried about missing a Sunday service here and there, which I never understood. He went to the semiannual church conferences but never sang in the choir, ushered, or played instruments. Yet, Andre was more Christ-like than I had ever been. He loved me and put his own desires on the back burner countless times to sacrifice for me (there was agape love again). He always listened to my concerns and showed compassion toward me when I was down. He was a man of integrity—as evidenced by getting married. He kept his word to me, even though it was an immature promise to begin with. So I could never call him a liar.

What was better: my lifelong church involvement and perfect attendance, or Andre's inconsistent church attendance but daily demonstration of Christ's spirit and love for others? As I learned more about God, I came to view my soon-to-be ex-husband as a modern example of how God wanted me to be. Here are a few characteristics I learned about God.

God is …

— **Willing to make sacrifices for you:** "For God so loved the world that He gave his only begotten Son" (John 3:16a)

— **Love:** "My beloved friends, let us continue to love each other since love comes from God. Everyone who loves is born of God and experiences a relationship with God. The person who refuses to love doesn't know the first thing about God, because God is love—so you can't know him if you don't love." (1 John 4:7–8, *The Message*)

- **Peaceful:** "Peace I leave with you, my peace I give unto you: not as the world giveth, give I unto you. Let not your heart be troubled, neither let it be afraid." (John 14:27)

- **Forgiving:** "For if ye forgive men their trespasses, your heavenly Father will also forgive you." (Matt. 6:14)

- **Even-tempered:** "The Lord is gracious, and full of compassion, slow to anger, and of great mercy." (Ps. 145:8)

- **A great provider:** "I have been young, and now I am old; yet I have not seen the righteous forsaken, nor his seed begging bread." (Ps. 37:25)

- **A safe haven:** "For in the time of trouble he shall hide me in his pavilion: in the secret of his tabernacle shall he hide me, he shall set me up upon a rock" (Ps. 27:5)

- **Honest:** "God is not a man, that he should lie; neither the son of man, that he should repent: hath he said, and shall he not do it? Or hath he spoken, and shall he not make it good?" (Num. 23:19)

More than ever, I began thanking God for my failed marriage, because I was being transformed into a better person, one to be used for God's works. It was almost like I was being saved again. I knew that if I put God first, my desires would eventually be fulfilled.

God's Dreams and Desires for Us

— **He wants to be first in our lives:** "Steep your life in God-reality, God-initiative, God-provisions. Don't worry about missing out. You'll find all your everyday human concerns will be met." (Matt. 6:33, *The Message*)

— **He wants us to praise him:** "From the lips of children and infants you have ordained praise." (Ps. 8:2)

— **He wants us to love him:** "Delight thyself also in the Lord; and He shall give thee the desires of thine heart." (Ps. 37:4)

— **He wants everyone in the world to be saved:** "… that whosoever believeth in him should not perish, but have everlasting life." (John 3:16b)

In this process of study, worship, reflection, and repentance, I developed a more intimate relationship with God. In fact, when I started thinking about all the promises God had made, I began falling in love. How could I *not* love someone who …

• Steers me in the right direction *(The Lord is my shepherd)*

• Supplies *all* of my needs *(I shall not want)*

• Knows when I need rest *(He maketh me to lie down in green pastures; He leadeth me beside the still waters)*

- Gives me strength *(He restoreth my soul)*

- Comforts me when I am afraid *(Yea, though I walk through the valley of the shadow of death, I shall fear no evil, for thou art with me, thy rod and thy staff, they comfort me)*

- Empowers me to overcome adversity *(Thou preparest a table before me in the presence of my enemies)*

- Blesses me *(Thou anointest my head with oil)*

- Provides abundant blessings *(My cup runneth over)*

- Gives me an unlimited number of second chances, and doesn't give me the penalties I deserve *(Surely goodness and mercy shall follow me all the days of my life)*

- Provides an uninterrupted presence *(And I will dwell in the house of the Lord)*

- Promises to never leave me *(Forever)* (Ps. 23)

To go further, God also …

- **Gives me power:** "But as many as received him, to them gave he power to become the sons of God, even to them that believe on his name." (John 1:12)

- **Gives me a peace of mind:** "For God hath not given us the spirit of fear; but of power, and of love, and of a sound mind." (2 Tim. 1:7)

- **Gives me hope:** "And let us not be weary in well doing: for in due season we shall reap, if we faint not." (Gal. 6:9)

- **Protects me:** "God is our refuge and strength, a very present help in trouble." (Ps. 46:1)

- **Is compassionate and faithful to me:** "Because of the Lord's great love we are not consumed, for his compassions never fail. They are new every morning; great is your faithfulness." (Lam. 3:22-23)

- **Knows my limitations:** "And God is faithful; he will not let you be tempted beyond what you can bear. But when you are tempted, he will also provide a way out so that you can stand up under it." (1 Cor. 10:13)

- **Filled in for my gaps:** "Likewise the Spirit also helpeth our infirmities: for we know not what we should pray for as we ought: but the Spirit itself maketh intercession for us with groanings which cannot be uttered." (Rom. 8:26)

- **Washed away my sins:** "To him give all the prophets witness, that through his name whosoever believeth in him shall receive remission of sins." (Acts 10:43)

- **Gives me confidence, encouragement, comfort, and strength:** "Now may our Lord Jesus Christ Himself and God our Father, Who loved us and gave us everlasting consolation and encouragement and well-founded hope through [His] grace (unmerited favor), comfort and encourage your hearts and strengthen them [make them steadfast and keep them unswerving] in every good work and word." (2 Thess. 2:16–17, *Amplified Bible*)

- **Provides abundant blessings across generations:** "If you listen obediently to the Voice of God, your God, and heartily obey all his commandments that I command you today, God, your God, will place you on high, high above all the nations of the world. All these blessings will come down on you and spread out beyond you because you have responded to the Voice of God, your God. God will lavish you with good things: children from your womb, offspring from your animals, and crops from your land, the land that God promised your ancestors that he would give you. God will throw open the doors of his sky vaults and pour rain on your land on schedule and bless the work you take in hand. You will lend to many nations but you yourself won't have to take out a loan. God will make you the head, not the tail; you'll always be the top dog, never the bottom dog, as you obediently listen to and diligently keep the commands of God, your God, that I am commanding you today. Don't swerve an inch to the right or left from the words that I command you today by going off following and worshiping other gods." (Deut. 28:1–2, 11–14, *The Message*)

To benefit from all of these promises, God only required that I "seek first the kingdom of God and all of His righteousness, and all these things shall be added unto you" (Matt. 6:33). This meant putting *him* first—not my business or job, not even my family, but God first! I was slowly beginning to understand why things turned out the way they did. I was seeking a husband first and God second. I was slowly starting to believe what I had been reading and studying, and many of these scriptures randomly popped into my mind, scriptures I had learned years ago. The Bible is true—you can read novels and autobiographies, short stories and thesis papers, but years later you probably won't remember them, and you definitely won't be able to quote them. On the other hand: "God's word will not return void" (Is. 55:11), and "the Holy Spirit will bring all things to your remembrance" (John 14:26). I learned so many of these scriptures through Sunday school, vacation Bible school, and church sermons, and years later, they were comforting and guiding me. Although I had been more caught up in religion rather than living in a Christ-like way, God's word and these lessons from my youth helped me tremendously.

In the span of three short years, I had become a mother and wife, and I had been separated and divorced, but an unexplainable peace came over me because I knew I would be fine. "My grace is sufficient for thee: for my strength is made perfect in weakness. Most gladly therefore will I rather glory in my infirmities, that the power of Christ may rest upon me" (2 Cor. 12:9). I was starting to praise God, even for the divorce.

On the day of our divorce, I had an "In-Dependence Day Celebration" with several girlfriends. It had less to do with the divorce and more to do with the growth I was experiencing and my new state of being—a state of dependence on God. Before, God had been my fifth priority, but no more. God would never again be relegated to second place. Here was the invitation I sent my friends:

To the Wonderful Women in My Life

When I was little, I used to believe in the concept of one best friend, and then I started to become a woman. And I found out that if you allow your heart to open up, God would show you the best in *many* best friends.

One friend when you are having man trouble. One friend when you are having family trouble. One friend when you want to shop, heal, hurt, joke, or just be. One friend to pray together, and another to laugh so hard that we cry together.

But whatever their assignment in our lives, on whatever occasions ... these are your best friends. We sometimes need friends with fresh perspectives, friends who will listen without judging. I thank you, my girlfriends, who honor intimacy, who hold trust, who always have my back when life is too heavy, as it has been for the past 12 months!

On the evening of my dissolution, come celebrate independence with me during dinner and salsa dancing. No, I'm not talking about independence from a husband or a marriage or bad choices, but join me to celebrate being in a state of *dependence* on God, who has been restored back to His rightful place in my life … #1.

Don't cry for me … sometimes we have to prune things in our lives before we can experience the growth that we're destined for … the life that was probably waiting for us all along. Let me celebrate the best in each of *you*—celebrate the things you've said or done, the ways you've believed in me, and the prayers you've uttered on my behalf during this unexpected time in my life. If you can't join in person, please join me in spirit and keep me in your prayers, especially on the day of my dissolution.

If I haven't said it before, I'll say it now. Thank you for being my friend, I love each of you.

That night we had a great time! A group of about eight friends went to dinner, where we had enlivening girl talk. Then we tried to go salsa dancing, but it had been cancelled that night, so we talked some more. Friends from around the country sent me encouraging words; I was encouraged by these messages of strength and hope and support.

From that day forward, I stopped worrying about how the story would end and started living according to God's will. I filled my mind with God's word (mostly through gospel music), I hung around other people who were living for God, and I started going with the flow instead of trying to control everything. I started enjoying every moment with my daughter and having lots of fun in the process. Most of all, I was more conscious about *whom* I was living for. I constantly checked my intentions to ensure that they were pure.

I felt at peace, but yet with a hopeful anticipation. Deep down inside, I had a feeling that God was going to do something extraordinary. I ran across a scripture one day that grabbed my attention. I quickly posted it on my bathroom mirror to encourage me every day: "Forget about what's happened; don't keep going over old history. Be alert, be present. I'm about to do something brand-new." (Is. 43:16, *The Message*)

Reflection Questions

1. What characteristics do you admire most about God?

_____

_____

_____

_____

_____

2. God has made countless promises to his children. Which promises are most inspiring to you?

_____

_____

_____

_____

_____

3. How can you demonstrate a state of in-dependence on God?

_____

_____

_____

_____

_____

Chapter 6

Selfishness and Love Can't Coexist

After almost thirty years of being a Christian, I was finally starting to follow the first Commandment—"Thou shall have no other gods before me" (Exod. 20:3). With nine commandments and an entire Bible to go, at the rate I was going, it's a wonder that God didn't give up on me! But I continued to study God's word. In the New Testament it said, "And thou shalt love the Lord thy God with all thy heart, and with all thy soul, and with all thy mind, and with all thy strength: this is the first commandment. And the second is like, namely this, Thou shalt love thy neighbour as thyself. There is none other commandment greater than these" (Mark 12:30–31). Wow! God doesn't want us to love just our neighbor—our fellow man, family, friends, enemies, co-workers, and loved ones—but ourselves as well!

At first glance, it may have seemed that I loved myself, but it didn't take long to figure out that I really didn't love myself as I should. I was nervous (my stubby, bitten nails served as proof all my life). I ignored my conscience (also known as the Holy Spirit), instead opting to do things on *my* terms in the way *I* wanted to do them. I didn't honor my temple, my body. I rarely exercised, didn't know how to cook, and frequently binged on sweets and treats. My habitual procrastination created a stressful life. Procrastination and lack of planning caused me to be late for nearly everything. I lived in cluttered spaces and didn't give myself room—or time—to breathe. It seemed like every corner of my house was crowded with a stack of papers, a knickknack, or some other unnecessary object. I also put so much pressure on myself to succeed that I failed to take time to relax, have fun, and just do nothing! I was running myself ragged.

I decided that enough was enough and decided to invest in myself. After all, my daughter was starting to emulate me, and I didn't want to be responsible for planting bad seeds that would eventually produce bad fruit. So I hired a caterer for private cooking lessons. She showed me how to prepare healthy dishes with flavor and how to plan meals. I tried several new fruits and vegetables so I could serve meals with good wholesome food, and I started cooking instead of eating out every day.

To get fit and healthy, I also hired a personal trainer. During the year that I trained, I really started to think—for the first time ever—that I was beautiful. Wow! I felt like a kid in a candy store. Not only was I starting to love my body—flaws and all—but I was starting to love myself. I was starting to "present my body as a living sacrifice, holy and acceptable unto God, which is your reasonable service" (Rom. 12:1).

Self love has less to do with getting a massage, fresh manicures, and a nice hairstyle, and more to do with honoring yourself by taking the time to relax, breathe, and think. It's about de-cluttering your environment to de-clutter your mind and making choices that honor your being while being true to yourself. Loving yourself is about being honest with yourself and being courageous enough to be honest with others, speaking the truth in love (Eph. 4:15), even when it may be difficult. It's about knowing your limitations but refusing to settle for less than what you're capable of so you might reach your full potential. Self love is accepting yourself for who and what you are. Without self love, there can be no foundation for a healthy marriage or any healthy relationship, because if you don't love yourself, you have absolutely no capacity to love others.

I learned even more about love during a workshop at my church. The English language has only one word for love; however, all love isn't created equal. The Greek language has different words for love: "eros" means erotic love; "phileo" means brotherly love; and "agape" means the love of God. Each form of love progresses in the level of intimacy, as the following illustration shows.

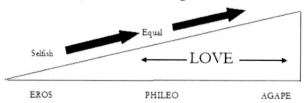

The word eros is not in the Bible; however, this English-derived word is an erotic type of love that is physical in nature. It is founded upon sensual, lustful passions and is the basis for prostitution, erotic dancing/stripping, pornography, and sexual immortality. The root of eros is selfishness, and it comes from Satan. In this type of love, the other person doesn't matter; all that matters is that *you* feel good. At the root of selfishness is fear, and God clearly states, "There is no fear in love. But perfect love drives out fear, because fear has to do with punishment. The one who fears is not made perfect in love" (1 John 4:18).

Phileo is brotherly, friendship love. The nature of phileo is about satisfaction. As long as things are going well, phileo love exists. However, when the level of satisfaction diminishes, so does the phileo. It's like saying, "If you love me, I'll love you" or "If you do for me, I'll do for you." Phileo is based on dependencies and qualifications, including how worthy the recipient is of your love, so this love can come and go.

It's easy to love those who love us back, but how can we love those who hate us or those who irritate us? This takes a special type of love, one that our humanity probably cannot achieve without God's help.

The highest and most intimate form of love is agape. It is the unmerited, unwarranted love of God. Unlike phileo, which is conditional, there are no prerequisites or qualifications one must meet in order to receive agape love. It isn't based on who *you* are or how *you* treat me. Rather, agape love is about who *I* am, the character of the person who is showing the love. Agape is the type of sacrificial, unyielding love that Jesus demonstrated by giving his very life, and God commands that we love each other the way he loves us. "Beloved, let us love one another: for love is of God; and every one that loveth is born of God, and knoweth God. He that loveth not knoweth not God; for God is love." (1 John 4:7–8) However, God goes a step further to say that we're not doing anything special to only love those who love us—we have to go above and beyond by loving and praying for God's blessings upon our enemies.

Here's another old saying that deserves a second look: "Eye for eye, tooth for tooth." Is that going to get us anywhere? Here's what I propose: "Don't hit back at all." If someone strikes you, stand there and take it. If someone drags you into court and sues for the shirt off your back, gift wrap your best coat and make a present of it. And if someone takes unfair advantage of you, use the occasion to practice the servant life. No more tit-for-tat stuff. Live generously.

You're familiar with the old written law, "Love your friend," and its unwritten companion, "Hate your enemy." I'm challenging that. I'm telling you to love your enemies. Let them bring out the best in you, not the worst. When someone gives you a hard time, respond with the energies of prayer, for then you are working out of your true selves, your God-created selves. This is what God does. He gives his best—the sun to warm and the rain to nourish—to everyone, regardless: the good and bad, the nice and nasty. If all you do is love the lovable, do you expect a bonus? Anybody can do that. If you simply say hello to those who greet you, do you expect a medal? Any run-of-the-mill sinner does that.

In a word, what I'm saying is, Grow up. You're kingdom subjects. Now live like it. Live out your God-created identity. Live generously and graciously toward others, the way God lives toward you. (Matt. 5:38–48, The Message)

Loving with agape love builds our character and allows Christ to show through us. God demonstrated this agape love toward us in the sacrifice of giving his only son to die a brutal and horrific death so that we could be saved. "For God so loved the world that He gave His only begotten son, that we might not perish, but have everlasting life. For God came not into the world to condemn the world, but that the world through Him might be saved" (John 3:16–17). God knew that we would sin and disappoint him time after time, yet he allowed his son to die for us! "While we were yet sinners, Christ died for us" (Rom. 5:8).

After learning about the three types of love, I felt like I'd been hit over the head with a ton of bricks. I realized how much turmoil the universal English word for love had caused in my relationship with Andre. It was now confirmed—I'd never practiced, nor really known, that agape love was the highest order and the standard for how to treat other people.

I found another reason for our failed marriage—Andre agape'd me, but I only phileo'd him. I said that I loved him, but I didn't show agape love in my actions. "My little children, let us not love in word, neither in tongue; but in deed and in truth" (1 John 3:18). Looking back, I realized that it was almost always about me—how I would feel and how a decision would affect me. I rarely, if ever, gave any thought to Andre's feelings, his perspective, or the impact decisions had on him. On the other hand, Andre would often go beyond the call of duty to show his love and allegiance for me, even after our divorce. For example, when I was running late to pick up our daughter, I would call Andre fifteen minutes before she needed to be picked up, tell a sob story about how I was running late, and ask him to pick her up instead. He would drop what he was doing and pick her up. Countless times in our marriage I forgot something that I needed from home—a document, something that needed to be faxed or mailed. Again, with a feeble tone of voice, I would call Andre to take care of it, and he would. No matter how inconvenient it was for him, Andre almost always came to my rescue, many times without complaint. In later years, Andre started to point out how insensitive it was to constantly depend on him to make up for my carelessness and inattentiveness. When the shoe was on the other foot, and he asked me to do something for him, I always evaluated the request in terms of my convenience, not his need. Although Andre willingly made sacrifices for me, I didn't have that same mindset.

I saw how phileo love manifested in other areas of my life besides our marriage, starting with something very basic—time. As I said before, I was a perpetual procrastinator and was always late. In my mind, being on time, let alone early, meant that I would "waste" my valuable time, and I didn't have a minute to waste. I soon realized that being late was actually rude to other people. It interrupted others who were on time, and it sent a message to the event leader and participants that I didn't value or honor them enough to be on time.

I also realized that I wasn't a very good listener and that I approached conversations and interactions with the secret intention of getting some benefit. My conversations were typically limited to generic questions like "How are you? Your spouse? Your children?" People often poured out their hearts to me—whether it was sharing an accomplishment or a struggle, a feeling or a dream—and failing to listen with my ears, eyes, and heart was disrespectful. Even in my business, my approach was all about what clients and business partners could do for me, not how I could serve them. I approached conversations with phileo love.

Although I was a master at phileo love, Andre, in contrast, always approached our relationship with agape. He always thought about me—sometimes to a fault, because he often neglected his own needs to make me happy. There are countless examples, the biggest of which was getting married. He followed through with the promise because he knew it would make me happy, even though he ended up being miserable. I interpreted that as being spoiled and adored by my husband, but it was really sacrificial, agape love. When Andre and I were together, we often had conversations about how far we would go to demonstrate our love for one another. "If we were in a sinking boat, I would save you. If we were in a cross fire, I'd take a bullet for you, Kristin," he told me. I shamefully admitted that I probably would be hesitant to do the same, but Andre had no hesitation. He epitomized the spirit of Christ: "Greater love hath no man than this, that a man lay down his life for his friends" (John 15:13).

All love isn't created equal, and one thing was for sure: I had a lot of growing—and confessing—to do.

Reflection Questions

1. How do you show that you love yourself?

_____

_____

_____

_____

_____

2. How have you shown phileo love? What is the impact on your relationships?

_____

_____

_____

_____

_____

3. How can you show agape love? What are your biggest challenges with showing agape love?

_____

_____

_____

_____

_____

Chapter 7

Acting, Doing, and Being

I mmediately after our divorce, I began to get in tune with my thoughts, feelings, and intentions—and I tuned Andre out, giving him the silent treatment for months. I was ashamed at the person who I'd become and the way that I'd treated him. I took an inventory on how I had become such a self-centered person. I don't think I made a conscious decision to be selfish and manipulative, but you never know. According to scientists, the average person has 12,000 thoughts per day, and a deeper thinker has more than 50,000 thoughts daily! Were there things I was thinking that I didn't realize? Did I unconsciously decide to be who I was?

Did I become selfish from being an only child? I didn't think I was spoiled, and other people usually were surprised that I was an only child, maybe because I didn't act like a spoiled brat who always wanted to have my way. Maybe I'd become this way from my days as a teacher's pet. I was always called on first to answer the questions, and I usually answered correctly. Over time, I began getting preferential treatment, and

I unconsciously decided that I would always be smart, I would always have the right answer, and therefore, I would always expect preferential treatment. This transcended into other areas of my life—the types of friends I chose, the relationships I engaged in, how I interacted in extracurricular school and church activities. I had to ensure that others would always see me as the smarter person who knew more. As an adult, I showed up as a self-righteous know-it-all, which made me feel powerful and privileged. This became my act—how I showed up to the world.

Thinking further, I had always been a leader in school and church, and at some point, I subconsciously decided to become a "savior"—I would always be there to save the day as the hero. It showed up in the friends I chose—I didn't hang out with my peers in the advanced classes; rather, I chose friends whose grades weren't as good as mine, friends who liked to hang out and sometimes even get into trouble. The guys I dated all had troubled pasts; perhaps I chose them because I felt like I could be a beacon of light to inspire them to do and be better. Even when Andre and I were married, I welcomed his then-twelve-year-old sister into our home when his mother suffered a debilitating stroke. When Andre moved out, I boldly declared that she didn't have to move back home; instead she could stay with me. After all, I felt like I was capable of "saving" her.

Just who did I think I was? Here I was, ragged and torn up myself, but focusing on trying to "save" someone else. I was the one who needed to be saved. I was starting to feel uneasy from this facade—I could keep up this act for only so long. I didn't want to live my entire life without feeling peace and contentment, loving myself, or learning how to truly love others.

I realized that I had become immersed in doing, doing, and more doing, just to keep up the act. I was *so* busy and *so* occupied, trying to look good to the world. Even when I had free time, I rarely, if ever, was content just sitting and being. I worried that if I stopped doing, perhaps I wouldn't accomplish my goals. It seemed like I had so much to prove, which is why I tended to do so much all the time. I realized that even in my marriage, I rarely spent time with my husband or daughter. I was too busy working and doing other things.

I wasn't alone. As a society, we're preoccupied with what we do. That's usually the first question I ask when I meet someone for the first time—"What do you do?" Although it's just an innocent conversation starter, the reality is that I often size up someone's worth, value, and benefit to me with the answer to this simple question. I decide whether I want to forge a relationship with them and whether the conversation will continue—or end—out of interest, or lack thereof. This, all from the simple question, "What do you do?"

I realized that I had become a human *doing* instead of a human *being*; I allowed my *doing* to define my *being*. We live in that type of society, though. Your profession, your appearance, the car you drive, the house you live in, the place you work, the way you speak, and how you dress all seem to define who you are. To keep up the act, be valuable to society, and look good to others, I stayed busy doing whatever it took, which led to a cycle of never-ending stress, poor self-esteem, suffering health, and a disconnect between my heart, mind, and actions. I believe that I stayed busy to avoid the pain of being alone.

I came to these realizations when I participated in a life-changing, three-day self-development course. After this awakening, I gave up doing as much as I'd done before and decided to just … *be*. It was a conscious decision. I wrote my thoughts in a journal so I could remember my intentions long after the feeling was gone. Instead of coming home from work and doing more work, I started doing homework with my daughter, watching TV, or talking on the phone with friends; I chose activities that were calming instead of stressful. I began reading again and even joined a book club to fellowship and have conversation with other women. Instead of staying up until the wee hours in the morning doing things, I began going to bed at reasonable hours so I could be well rested and energetic the next day.

Thinking back to this transformation, I identified five principles that guided how I started to live a powerful and engaging life:

1) Be present in each moment. I was quick to multitask. It almost became a necessary evil. I talked on the phone while driving. I watched TV while folding the clothes. I checked email while talking on the phone. And the list goes on. Although multitasking definitely has its place, at times I needed to stop multitasking and focus on being present. Believe it or not, I actually got *more* done when I was focused on the task, instead of spreading my attention. My conversations were more powerful and meaningful when I was listening with intent, and the other people in the conversations felt like they were the most important person in the world. They knew that I was fully present. I tuned out the world and focused on them. I really listened to what people were saying, instead of thinking about what I would say next.

2) Be a person of your word, a person of integrity. There was a saying several years ago, "Word is bond." That's a very powerful thing, when your word is your bond, or your promise, oath, and pledge. This is the essence of integrity.

When I traveled to Africa several years ago, I learned firsthand what it means when your word is your bond. Walking through the market, the shop owners would ask me to come to their shop and look around. I'd respond almost automatically, "Sure, I'll come back later." Well, later came, and they saw me again. "Sister, sister, you said that you would come to my shop. Why don't you come?" I had to go at that point because I'd made a promise, and they were counting on me. I realized at that moment just how much I broke promises. I'd say I would call people back, and I promised to keep in touch with friends, but I often didn't. I had gotten really good at making commitments that I didn't keep, probably because I was so busy acting and doing.

A friend described it like this: "Integrity is doing what you said you would do, *long* after the feeling under which you said it has gone." That's really profound.

I often made promises when the energy was high and I was excited and optimistic in the moment, but after that moment was gone and the enthusiasm dissipated, I was left uninspired to follow through. I learned that integrity means following through with what you've said, *no matter what!*

3) Be fully self-expressed. I recently read a book about the differences between men and women, one of which is how differently we communicate. When something bothered me in my marriage, Andre would ask, "What's wrong?" I'd reply, "Nothing." "Are you sure? It seems like something's up with you." I knew something was wrong, but I didn't want to admit it because it might have made me look bad, which would have been inconsistent with my act. So I suppressed my feelings, but inside, I didn't feel at ease because I wasn't being totally honest with Andre or myself.

Beyond the relationship, this principle applied at home, at work, at church, and in the community. We were going through an acquisition at work that was physically and emotionally draining. Merging two multi-billion-dollar companies and combining two different teams with varying styles, personalities, intentions, and goals proved to be very challenging. Many times, instead of addressing the entire team, we would murmur and complain among ourselves to avoid disrupting the flow of the meeting and any progress we were making. However, I felt that we were inhibiting our leadership team's progress with side conversations instead of facing the reality of the business situation, people's beliefs, and feelings head on—as a team. While others shied away from being outspoken, I boldly stated what many thought and talked about in private because, in reality, it *was* causing lack of unity among our team. I liberated myself because I talked about what needed to be said.

Being fully self-expressed opened me up for greatness and also prevented me from that imbalanced feeling of uneasiness. If I had not talked honestly with Andre and my co-workers, if I had not written in my journal and talked to God, suppressing my feelings could have led to a physical or emotional disease.

4) Be authentic. Be authentic by being genuine. Have genuine care and concern for people. Be authentic by being yourself, by giving up your act. I became authentic by telling the truth, and the truth set me free! When I had that queasy feeling in my stomach, it usually meant that something was wrong. Several times I made commitments to Andre, for example, to pick up our daughter from his house at a certain time. I knew I was stretching myself too thin by not allotting enough time in between my commitment and picking her up. So instead of being too optimistic and not being a person of my word like I had been so many times before, I was authentic and accountable. I admitted that I was being too aggressive, and I pushed back the pickup time.

I was also authentic and honest with myself. When I was so outspoken during the blending of our two teams at work, my intentions weren't always pure. I wasn't a fan of the new team leader, and sometimes I made comments just to make him look bad. Although I was proud of myself for being courageous enough to speak aloud what others had thought and talked about privately, at times I also felt uneasy about my motives. I began to acknowledge this—the disrespect I was showing to the leader, the example I was setting for the team members who reported to me, and the atmosphere it created in our leadership team. After much prayer and humbling myself, I put my ego aside and acknowledged my wrongdoing to the team leader, and I even asked for forgiveness. Although the conversation was difficult, afterward I felt liberated.

5) Be a person of love. I had this aha moment during another self-development workshop. It was a ten-week course about living more powerfully. The course included teaching, discussion, life application, and testimony. For ten weeks, I spent three hours a week getting to know people from all walks of life—men and women; young and old; rich and poor; black, white, Asian and Latino; entrepreneurs and people who were unemployed; and on and on. Never before had I really gotten to know people who weren't like me, particularly people who weren't Black.

Throughout my life, I had always hung around other African-Americans. In choosing a college, I even had a criterion that I attend a historically black college or university because I believed that only black people had my best intentions at heart. My friends were always Black. The people I admired were Black. I even visited Africa multiple times to prove how "Black" I was! In my heart, I believed that White people wanted Blacks to fail and were conspiring against us and, therefore, couldn't be trusted. I also believed that White people were more privileged and didn't have as many problems as Black people did. My mom often told me, "You have to be twice as good to get half as far." She wasn't alone in that belief. This is a common saying in the African-American community because we believe that the "system" is set up against us, which I no longer endorse or believe.

Getting to know this diverse group of people in the workshop helped me understand that although we may differ in our gender, ethnicity, origin, language, and beliefs, at the core of the human spirit, we're all just *people*. We all have problems and insecurities. We all want to be loved, and we all want to be valued for our contributions to the world. When we are and show agape love, we simultaneously show our humanity and our divinity. So although my ethnicity and heritage is an undeniable piece of who I am, I decided to be more human than I am Black, more human than I am woman, more human than I am American. Instead of assuming racial discrimination was behind every ill in society between Black and White people, I started looking at the heart of the matter as *people*. I started loving people as *people*.

In the past, I had gotten gratification from acting and doing, but the real power was in *being*. Although it took an extra effort to force myself to be, it didn't take much extra time, and the benefits were priceless! I practiced being with my daughter, co-workers, and even with Andre, and it was working because they felt like I was fully in tune with them in that moment! I realized I could reinvent my life with my thoughts and words. "Be ye transformed by the renewing of your mind" (Rom. 12:2). I started to reinvent my relationship with Andre by reinventing my act—how I presented myself to him based on who I decided I would be. I had spent my entire life acting and doing, and although I couldn't transform into a human *being* overnight, I was enjoying the process.

Reflection Questions

1. Is there consistency between how you act, what you do, and who you are? Explain.

_____

_____

_____

_____

_____

2. What type of person do you choose to be?

_____

_____

_____

_____

_____

3. List two or three instances in your life that have made you who you are.

_____

_____

_____

_____

_____

Chapter 8

Birthing Pains

January 1, 2006

"Happy New Year! What a year 2005 proved to be! A year of loss and a year of gains. I lost a husband but gained a friend. I lost sense of control but gained the will of God. I lost money in real estate but gained being debt free from credit cards. I lost some of my pride but gained resilience. I lost arrogance but gained humility. But I haven't lost weight yet. That's coming next year!

All jokes aside, what a year this has been! Thank you, God, for keeping my mind; for mending my broken heart; for removing the things—and people—that separated me from you. Through all the loss, you have kept my mind focused and calm. What a blessing to know you and love you, and moreover, for you to love a wretch like me. I used to turn my nose up to that phrase in the song "Amazing Grace"—"that saved a wretch like me"—but I have certainly done some wretched things of which I am truly ashamed. But, through all of these circumstances, you have never left my side, and I am ever so grateful.

Who knows what you have in store for next year or the future? Whatever it is, I make myself available and stand ready not only to receive blessings, but also to receive your discipline, guidance, assurance, safety, chastisement, and love. I desire to love you more than I love myself and more than I've ever claimed to love Andre. I desire to love without inhibition. I desire to let your ways be my ways and your thoughts my thoughts.

This is a significant year. My life changed so dramatically since seven years ago when I started dating Andre. Back then, I glowed, I was happy, I was unstoppable, and my happiness couldn't be contained. I thought I loved Andre, but what I enjoyed most was being loved by him. Our romantic relationship had flawed beginnings and a bitter ending, yet I have grown tremendously. I know, without a doubt, that it has all been for a divine purpose. It has—and will—all work together for my good. And in this seventh year since meeting Andre, you revealed, Lord, that this is the year of completion, the time to perfect yourself in us and manifest yourself through us.

Thank you, God. I now want you to be all that Andre was to me and more. Make me whole, fill my cup, reassure my insecure mind, and love me even when I'm not lovable. And I know that when I put you first, all these things shall be added unto me. Yes, I want a husband—someone to share my life with—and I want more children, and I want to travel and do so many other things. But first, I want to be like you, pattern myself after you, and let you teach me how to love. Only then could I be ready for anyone else.

I'm excited about taking my life back—the personal training, intentional eating, conscious relaxation, and disciplined thinking. Thanks for not giving up on me, God, and for making me resilient.

In love,

- Krissy

I was really pleased with the progress I'd made in being honest with myself, taking bold steps to forgive, and correcting my wicked ways. But, I needed to do something else. It wasn't enough to forgive myself—I also had to confess to and ask forgiveness from Andre. Many times, writing letters was the easiest way to express myself, and this time was no different.

January 6, 2006

Dear Andre,

I'm writing to you after the first day of this self-development workshop. I've learned a few things about my past that I want to take responsibility for, and I'm writing to you because I'm committed to our growth and development, to healing and wholeness, and to the revelations that come in the process.

In the workshop, one of the possibilities I created was the possibility of being open to the natural flow and process of life. I realized that I wasn't honest or authentic in some aspects of our relationship. I pretended that if we weren't together I wouldn't be able to live without you. I pretended not to be hurt by actions that caused deep pain for both of us. I pretended to love you fully and completely, when in reality, my love for you was scattered with selfishness.

Acting this way made me feel like I was right—and you were wrong. I dominated you instead of allowing you to love me and willingly accepting your love for me. I used it as a way to validate my self-worth, when it was really a cover up for not loving myself. And I had to win at all costs. I realize that I really loved the feeling of keeping you wrapped around my finger, instead of loving you.

It cost me a lot. It cost me love. I couldn't possibly treat you this way and love you at the same time. It cost trust, our marriage, embarrassment, and unhappiness for both of us. I acknowledge this and am deeply regretful.

So I'm letting life flow naturally instead of being controlling and thinking that I need to save you or the world.

Kris

I came home from the seminar and immediately called Andre to read this letter. He was speechless! He couldn't believe these words were coming out of my mouth. Very rarely, if ever, had I confessed wrongdoings to him before. But today was different. My freedom was dependent on confession, forgiveness, and repentance. It didn't matter that we were divorced—I needed to make things right with him. I felt so liberated expressing myself to Andre that I wrote a letter to myself the next night.

> Dear Krissy,
>
> You know as well as I know that you haven't told the truth. You tell the truth only when there is some revelation or insightful nugget that makes you look like a hero. Stop fooling yourself! Don't you know that you'd feel much more liberated if you just got in tune with your feelings—in each moment—and were straight up? Face the brutal facts, stop holding yourself hostage, and start living!
>
> You came to this seminar to have an epiphany, and you realized that you're close-minded and judgmental, the very same qualities you despise in others. In the process, you've acknowledged that incompetencies and flaws do, in fact, exist in your life, but in the acknowledgement, they have now disappeared. How miraculous! By admitting—instead of ignoring—your shortcomings, they no longer plague you! Why didn't you

let go of these years ago and stop giving them power over you?

So, your new possibilities include being whole and complete; being worthy of love; being lovable; and accepting love as much as you give it to others. You're considerate of other people's time and feelings. And most of all, you've created the possibility of letting life flow instead of controlling everything—and nothing—all at the same time. You've given up relying on the stories of your past that prove you were imperfect, vulnerable, and unworthy; and instead, you're now living each moment within itself, unconstrained by pretenses and in-authenticities.

Here's to your new life ... a new year ... and a new you!

Your friend and honest confidante,

Kristin

You can't change what you won't acknowledge, and now that I had confessed—both to myself and Andre—asked for forgiveness, and repented, the universe seemed to open up. I confronted my enemies, including the enemy "in-a-me." I had been honest about my fears—living a life of searching for, but never finding love; feeling embarrassed in front of other people; being a failure; not mattering to people; and worrying that my past would limit my future. Although fear is a very real emotion, letting it dominate and control me didn't seem right. So I searched the Bible for passages on fear. Overall, most passages discussed fearing the

Lord, not people, perceptions, or my own insecurities. Maybe if I were fearful of God, I wouldn't have time or energy to be fearful of man? In my search, two messages stood out to me:

1. In the presence of love, fear disappears, and if you're fearful, love can't exist. "Since fear is crippling, a fearful life—fear of death, fear of judgment—is one not yet fully formed in love" (1 John 4:19).

2. If I wanted to be wise or smart, I needed to start by fearing God and stop fearing man. This scripture showed up several times in the Bible:

- "The fear of the Lord is the beginning of wisdom: a good understanding have all they that do his commandments: his praise endureth forever." (Ps. 111:10)

- "The fear of the Lord is the beginning of knowledge: but fools despise wisdom and instruction." (Prov. 1:7)

- "The fear of the Lord is the beginning of wisdom: and the knowledge of the holy is understanding." (Prov. 9:10)

I was beginning to more fully trust in God instead of depending only on what I could understand. I loved God with all my heart, mind, and soul, and although I still desired to be happily married in the future, one day God whispered something to me that changed my mindset forever. *"How can you be trusted with a man if you can't even take care of what you have now?"* Whew! I felt like I'd been whipped upside the head again! It was true. My house was always a mess, I rarely spent time relaxing or having fun—even with my daughter—and I didn't cook regularly. It made sense. I had to get my *own* house in order before inviting someone else into it. After all, I wouldn't have a house party and neglect to clean up!

From that day forward, I was more conscious about making sure my house was clean—both my physical house and my temple—my body, soul, and mind. Almost every night, I took ten to fifteen minutes to straighten up my house. Instead of listening to the radio, which often aired destructive messages, I listened to gospel music to keep my mind focused on God on my way to and from work. I started spontaneously dancing with my daughter in the middle of the living room, just to have fun and spend time together. It was also a fun workout that didn't feel like exercise! The scripture reinforced God's whisper: "Well done, thou good and faithful servant: thou hast been faithful over a few things, I will make thee ruler over many things" (Matt. 25:21).

I kept hearing a scripture in gospel music and at concerts … *"speak those things that be not as though they were."* In the Bible, it actually reads, "… gives life to the dead and speaks of the nonexistent things that He has foretold and promised, as if they already existed." (Rom. 4:17b, *21st Century King James Version*) So, instead of waiting for another marriage so I could become a great wife, I began acting as though it were already done! I started cooking, cleaning, and spending time with my daughter. Instead of being so uptight and stressed out, I started having spontaneous fun—dancing in the living room and playing in the snow. I was calling into being what didn't previously exist.

My first marriage was built on a sinking foundation of pride, selfishness, and incongruent beliefs and actions, but I was determined that the next marriage—if there was to be one—would be built on a solid foundation. More than twenty years after learning this song during vacation Bible school, it still rung in my ears:

> Don't build your house on a sandy land
> Don't build it too near the shore
> Well, it might look kind of nice, but you'll have
>   to build it twice
> And you'll have to build your house once more.
> You'd better build your house upon a rock.
> Make a good foundation on a solid spot.
> Well, the storms may come and go,
> But the peace of God you will know.

That song was based on Psalm 127:1, which reads "Except the Lord build the house, they labour in vain that build it: except the Lord keep the city, the watchman waketh but in vain."

As I began to emerge from these deep reflections and started communicating with Andre again, our friendship began to re-emerge. We started hanging out together and going to community events and after-five galas together. Our friends would see us out together and privately ask again if we were really separated. "Yes, we're actually divorced," we would say, and they would walk away baffled at how an ex-husband and ex-wife could *possibly* be friends. It seemed out of the realm of possibility for so many; but friendship was the foundation of our relationship. Even when we separated, I prayed that our friendship would remain, and God was faithful. We stayed friends, even through the bitterness of divorce.

The tongue is one of the smallest parts of the body but, by far, the most powerful. "Words kill, words give life; they're either poison or fruit—you choose" (Prov. 18:21, *The Message*). The lyrics to one of the songs from our wedding had set the tone: "I won't harm you with words from my mouth, I love you, I need you to survive" (as sung by Hezekiah Walker). Years after the wedding, we had resisted the temptation to talk down about each other to our friends and family, because the seed had been planted that we wouldn't harm each other with our words.

My words—and actions—were slowly starting to demonstrate the change in my heart and mind, and I was thankful that new seeds—ones of forgiveness, peace, and joy—were taking root and bearing good fruit. "You don't get wormy apples off a healthy tree, nor good apples off a diseased tree. The health of the apple tells the health of the tree. You must begin with your own life-giving lives. It's who you are, not what you say and do, that counts. Your true being brims over into true words and deeds" (Luke 6:43–45, *New American Standard Bible*). I also like the translation which says, "for out of the abundance of the heart his mouth speaks" (Luke 6:45, *Amplified Bible*).

Certainly those nine to twelve months after our divorce were painful—admitting to the wickedness that was in my heart, confessing my wrongdoings to Andre, asking forgiveness, and repenting. I cried myself to sleep on more nights than I can count, and I suffered silently in anguish, but for some reason, I knew that on the other side of the labor pains was the birth of something miraculous and beautiful. I had absolutely no logical reason to feel this, but I had faith and belief that my life was *exactly* the way that God intended it to be. I believed that, somehow, all of this would work out for my good. After all, that's what God promised in Romans 8:28. I didn't know what, why, how, or when, but I was going along for the ride. Just like any road trip or roller-coaster ride, there were ups and downs. Suffering was definitely part of my journey, and I had my share of labor pains in the process of giving birth to my potential.

All around us we observe a pregnant creation. The difficult times of pain throughout the world are simply birth pangs. But it's not only around us, it's within us. The Spirit of God is arousing us within. We're also feeling the birth pangs. These sterile and barren bodies of ours are yearning for full deliverance. That is why waiting does not diminish us, any more than waiting diminishes a pregnant mother. We are enlarged in the waiting. We, of course, don't see what is enlarging us. But the longer we wait, the larger we become, and the more joyful our expectancy.

Meanwhile, the moment we get tired in the waiting, God's Spirit is right alongside helping us along. If we don't know how or what to pray, it doesn't matter. He does our praying in and for us, making prayer out of our wordless sighs, our aching groans. He knows us far better than we know ourselves, knows our pregnant condition, and keeps us present before God. That's why we can be so sure that every detail in our lives of love for God is worked into something good.

God knew what he was doing from the very beginning. He decided from the outset to shape the loves of those who love him along the same lines as the life of his Son. The Son stands first in the line of humanity he restores. We see the original and intended shape of our lives there in him. After God made that decision of what his children should be like, he followed it up by calling people by name. After he called them by name, he set them on a solid basis with himself. And then, after getting them established, he stayed with them to the end, gloriously completing what he had begun.

So, what do you think? With God on our side like this, how can we lose? "All around us we observe a pregnant creation. The difficult times of pain throughout the world are simply birth pangs. But it's not only around us; it's within us. The Spirit of God is arousing us within. We're also feeling the birth pangs. These sterile and barren bodies of ours are yearning for full deliverance. That is why waiting does not diminish us, any more than waiting diminishes a pregnant mother. We are enlarged in the waiting. We, of course, don't see what is enlarging us. But the longer we wait, the larger we become, and the more joyful our expectancy." (Rom. 8:22–25, *The Message*)

Reflection Questions

1. Are there sins that you need to confess, seek forgiveness for, and repent to someone else or yourself?

_____

_____

_____

_____

_____

2. God commands that we take care of what we have before he can trust us with more. Of what do you need to be a better steward?

_____

_____

_____

_____

_____

3. In the past, how has God transformed something that could have been bad in order to work for your good?

_____

_____

_____

_____

Chapter 9

With or Without You

As controlling as I had been, I realized that God was truly in control. One beautiful thing about God is that he allows us to have free will—to make choices. However, when he wants to teach us a lesson, we *will* learn it, whether we want to or not. We can learn through joy, or we can learn through pain, but we *will* learn the lesson. I could have very easily just listened to God during the engagement and called off the wedding—but no, I was stubborn, and I had to have my way. All I had dreamed about was being a wife, mother, business owner, and an involved community member, and it had all come to pass, but neither Andre nor I was truly happy. The weekend of my birthday was a point of reckoning when I had to decide if I wanted to continue on this destructive path or correct the error of my ways. I chose the latter and spent months focusing on repenting and being healed.

The New Testament recounts several instances of Jesus healing people of their ailments, but what's so interesting is that all of the people were healed *differ-*

ently. In Matthew 8:1–3, a leper came to Jesus on his hands and knees, begging to be healed, and with one touch from Jesus, he was cleansed. In Matthew 8:5–13, a Roman captain came to Jesus on behalf of one of his servants who couldn't walk and was in grave pain. Jesus volunteered to go to his home to heal the servant, but the captain pleaded with Jesus: "Just say the word and my servant will be healed" (Matt. 8:8, *NIV*). Although the servant was far away, Jesus was so impressed with the master's faith that he healed the servant that very hour—long distance! In another instance of healing, a woman who had been hemorrhaging blood for twelve years was so desperate for God's healing that she believed touching Jesus's robe would heal her. Again, Jesus recognized her faith, and healed her (Matt. 9:20–22).

Whether the afflicted were healed because of their requests or the intercession of others, the consistent thread was faith; they were all healed because of their belief in God's ability to heal. However, sometimes our faith needs to be increased before we can be healed. This is illustrated in John 9, where Jesus healed a man who had been blind from birth. The people asked Jesus who in the family had committed a sin to cause this man to be blind. Jesus scolded them, telling them not to look for anyone to blame; rather, he instructed them to focus on what Jesus could *do*. This is a salient point—it's so much easier to place blame than to accept the situation as it is, without logic or reason. But Jesus wants us to know that everything that happens in life *is supposed to happen exactly like this.*

Jesus also healed another blind man, but unlike the

other healings, he made the man participate in his own healing. Jesus spit into the dirt and made a clay paste to put on the man's eyes, and then he directed him to go to the Pool of Siloam, which was some distance away, to wash his eyes. The blind man had to travel, probably by himself, in order to be healed; but it was all a part of the journey.

Just like the blind man at the Pool of Siloam, I had to participate in my own healing. Getting married, separated, and divorced was absolutely necessary for my healing. After all, I didn't agape Andre, and I certainly didn't appreciate the husband God had blessed me with. Instead of asking why all of this happened, I began focusing on how I could be healed. The answer was simple—"Trust in the Lord with all thine heart, and lean not unto thine own understanding. In all thy ways acknowledge Him and he shall direct thy path" (Prov. 3:4–5).

When you confront your past and heal from it, you claim your future. As I was being healed, my friendship with Andre was also being restored; in fact, we became better friends after we divorced than we'd ever been while we were dating or married. After I stopped being bitter and angry about the divorce, we stopped picking up and dropping off our daughter as if it were a business transaction. Instead we used it as an opportunity to talk to each other again. We asked how each other's day was, listened without interrupting or multitasking, and began spending time together—albeit ten minutes to start—talking, watching TV, or doing nothing at all. We were truly enjoying each other's friendship, and we even started dating again! This time, though, we didn't have any self-imposed deadlines, and I wasn't driving toward a goal of getting married, although, in my heart, I desired that we would be reunited one day.

Things were going so well in our newfound relationship! We talked about getting married and being a family again; we looked at rings; and we even talked about the logistics of housing—who would move and what we'd do with the other house. But there came a time during that year when Andre experienced a significant amount of stress and reneged on the conversations we'd had only weeks prior about getting married again. I was in shock, but I did my best to stay calm. *"He is going through a stressful time right now,"* I thought to myself. *"So I'll give him a few weeks to think this over while he's with his family for the holidays, but when he comes back in town and we have this conversation, that's it. We're either going to be together or not. I will* not *put myself through any more emotional turmoil, and I will not make the same mistake twice."* I had this same conversation with Andre, and, as promised, I gave him a few weeks to think things over.

I'd made ultimatums before, but this time it wasn't an empty promise or threat. I was deadly serious about not bringing any more suffering or anguish into my life. In fact, for the first time in my life, I could honestly say that I could go on with—or without—Andre. After rereading what I'd written in my journal months and years ago and reconnecting with the pain that I experienced and the person that I had become, I decided that I would have a wonderful life and be happy, even if I never married anyone again. What was most important to me was living a fulfilled life that pleased God, a life filled with peace, passion, purpose, and strong connections with people. That type of life was available to me whether or not I was married. I couldn't believe it! Was this the same Kristin whose biggest fear was living life alone and never getting married again?

"Submit to God and be at peace with Him. In this way, prosperity will come to you. Accept instruction from his mouth and lay up his words in your heart" (Job 22:21–22). The split second I made that decision and declaration, fear was eliminated, and the situation changed. Miraculously, my fear of being alone for the rest of my life was gone! I was at peace with God—and with whatever the outcome was going to be. It wasn't until I let go of my fear that I made room for blessings.

At least three weeks passed since Andre and I had the initial "ultimatum" conversation, and he still hadn't given me an answer. So I took his lack of response as a sign that he didn't want to be together and decided to move on with my life. I went to another self-development course where I learned how destructive it is to put my ego and pride ahead of honesty, integrity, and personal growth. I realized how much ego I really had—it showed up as self-righteousness, judgment, fear, and living with selfish intentions. The only way to overcome ego was forgiveness, and that weekend, I forgave Andre—and myself—once again. I resolved to live with honesty, integrity, and free of my ego! This was a timely lesson.

The weekend after I returned from the workshop, I decided to go to my favorite party. I only went to one party in the city; they played my favorite music from the '80s and '90s, the atmosphere was intimate, and the crowd was filled with intelligent people. I made a point to go nearly every month—even if I went by myself—because I had so much fun! Typically, Andre kept our daughter on those Saturday nights, but this weekend, she was with my parents. Eager to have fun, I entered the party, and guess who was there? Andre. At that time, one of the most popular songs was "Irreplaceable" by Beyonce, which asserted that no man was irreplaceable. The song was blaring from the speakers, and I could see Andre looking at me sing the lyrics with passionate agreement. "I could see you from across the room—I know you're singing about me," he said. "You're right," I replied.

Talking about the situation later, I confessed to Andre that he was *not* irreplaceable. I was only singing that song to ease my pain. (There's proof—the tongue can be so wicked!) It was ludicrous to think that I could find another "him" in a minute, or any period of time, for that matter. As nice as it sounds to quickly get over someone who's hurt you, people just aren't replaceable, and Andre was certainly one of a kind. We say things like that to make it seem like we don't have feelings and that others can't hurt our feelings. But Andre knew I was serious about the finality of this decision to either be together or not.

That night we talked at length about our failed marriage and the flaws and insecurities that had led to its demise. We talked about the pain we'd felt and the impact it had on our daughter. Andre acknowledged that the grass wasn't always greener on the other side, and that, regardless of my flaws, no other woman could come close to me. We talked about how great it would be to be a family again. We removed any pretenses and expressed our undying love for each other, nearly eighteen months after our divorce. We promised that we would agape love each other and bar selfishness and bitterness from our hearts. There was no denying that we were meant to be, and that night we mutually decided to be together … forever.

Reflection Questions

1. What is necessary in order for you to be healed?

_____

_____

_____

_____

_____

2. What is your biggest fear? Will you allow God to free you from that fear?

_____

_____

_____

_____

_____

3. What's the worst that could happen if you were totally honest about your situation?

_____

_____

_____

_____

_____

Chapter 10

The God of a Second Chance

"And we know that all things work together for the good of those who love the Lord and are called according to His purpose."

(Rom. 8:28)

I once had a poverty mindset when it came to love. I once believed that love was scarce and there wasn't enough to go around. I believed that in order to show dedication, I had to ignore everything and everyone else and only choose one. When we confess our sins and give our lives to Christ, we enter into a covenant agreement to serve God and live for him the rest of our lives. Take a marriage between a man and a woman— you make a commitment to love only your spouse. Based on these rules, I somehow believed that I had to choose between God or my spouse, my child or my work. This was a poverty mentality based on lack and scarcity. However, God demonstrates time and time again just how plentiful his blessings are.

God shows us that we should live in abundance, not

lack! In fact, he created a covenant to love and forgive millions of people. God doesn't direct his love to only one person at a time. Rather, he loves more people than you or I could ever count—in fact, every single person in world. It's been like this since the beginning of time. Further, he loves each of us exactly the same and gives no favor to any man. "For there is no respect of persons with God" (Rom. 2:11). Regardless of who we are, what we do, what we say, or how we act, God continues to love us. After all, his agape love is not based on us; it's based on God's character. "I've never quit loving you and never will. Expect love, love, and more love!" (Jer. 31:3, *The Message*). More than ever, I was in love with God, and although I had to "share" him with countless other people, in the personal and intimate relationship I had with God, it felt like I was the only one. In the same way, we are required to love everyone—our neighbor and ourselves out of the abundance of our hearts, not the lack. I learned that it's possible to love and serve God and still love your family, friends, and others at the same time.

Although God commands us to love everyone just like he loves us, God wants to have a special place in our hearts for him. God is a jealous God and demands to be first in our lives. Putting God first doesn't mean that I need to spend one hundred hours a week in prayer, meditation, and Bible study. Rather, putting God first means that I live my very life for God. It means that I love people and show them kindness. It means I love people wholly and put my ego aside. When I do wrong, being Christ-like (which is the meaning of my birth name) means to repent and ask forgiveness, instead of insisting on being right and making someone else wrong.

My first marriage to Andre had to end so I could realize that it was separating me from God's love. I was demonstrating spiritual infidelity and literally cheating on God. I cheated by ignoring the Holy Spirit's guidance and instead doing whatever I wanted to do, when and how I wanted to do it. During my first marriage, I prioritized God behind nearly everything and everyone else—my job and business, my husband, and my child. I didn't love them with God's agape love or look for opportunities to demonstrate God's love to them through my actions. I didn't take time to build my relationship with God and love him even more deeply. During the separation and divorce, I learned that I had to love God even more than my husband; after all, that is the first commandment. As a secondary priority, God says that we should love our neighbors, including our spouse, as ourselves. In loving others, we actually demonstrate our love for God.

With God as my number-one priority, I now had room to love others, including myself. Andre and I started spending time together as a couple and as a family with our daughter. I was able to love Andre more purely and generously because I wasn't focused on choosing between either God or Andre; rather, I was able to love them both! Andre and I even went on a couples' retreat at our church. There we learned that love is the foundation for a healthy marriage. God speaks countless times of the importance of love, both for God and each other.

- "And now these three remain: faith, hope and love. But the greatest of these is love." (1 Cor. 13:13, *NIV*)

- "Love each other as if your life depended on it. Love makes up for practically anything." (1 Peter 4:8, *The Message*)

- "A new commandment I give unto you, that ye love one another; as I have loved you, that ye also love one another. By this shall all men know that ye are my disciples, if ye have love one to another." (John 13:34)

- "If anyone boasts, 'I love God,' and goes right on hating his brother or sister, thinking nothing of it, he is a liar. If he won't love the person he can see, how can he love the God he can't see? The command we have from Christ is blunt: Loving God includes loving people. You've got to love both." (1 John 4:20–21, *The Message*)

I was learning so much about love that I became excited about life and being able to demonstrate my newfound standard of love—agape. It was like a dream come true that Andre and I would one day again be united in marriage, something I had only wished for and cried for on so many nights. "Ask for whatever you wish and I will give it to you for God's glory" (John 14:13).

More than ever, I was convinced that all of these circumstances happened so I could tell of God's miraculous power. Andre and I had already decided that we would get married again, and we even started marital counseling. We didn't get counseling before the first marriage, but we both wanted to do things the right way this time. The counseling sessions went well, and we received the minister's agreement that we were adequately prepared to be married. But I didn't want to use the same ring from the first marriage because I felt like it carried too much negative baggage. So Andre committed to saving up money to buy another ring. A couple of months later he said, "You know, the only thing stopping us from getting married is a ring. Why not just use the one we have, and I'll buy another one later?" He had always been a visionary, and it made a lot of sense. This marriage wasn't about a new ring, a fancy wedding, or hosting hundreds of guests—it was for *us*. It was a Monday night, and we decided to get married that Friday in May—why wait? I called my uncle, who was our pastor at the time, and asked if he was available that Friday evening. He was. Just like that, we were on our way to being wedded again.

Andre and I had a sunset wedding at our favorite local park three-and-a-half years after we'd first said "I do," and nearly two years after our divorce. The ceremony was eight minutes long. There were only two guests—our daughter and my aunt. There was no music, no fanfare, and no stress. It was truly the *most* beautiful wedding. It wasn't about fancy rituals. What was most important was the covenant we made with God. Unlike the first marriage, this time God had joined us together, and no one could put it asunder (Mark 10:9).

Maybe that's why more than one in two marriages in the United States ends in divorce—because God hasn't joined them together. I wasn't making the same mistakes twice, and I approached the marriage and wedding ceremony with an excited, yet serious mood. After all, marriage is a lifelong commitment that shouldn't be entered into lightly.

As I was writing this book, I had a major revelation. We were married—for the second time—on May 11, three years from the day we had decided to separate! How amazing! Obviously, it wasn't planned that way, because we spontaneously decided on a Monday to get married that Friday. That's a modern-day miracle and an example of how the spirit of God works, bringing things into being that we don't even realize for his purpose and glory.

After we got married, I didn't send out a blast email, nor did I have a phone telethon to tell all of my friends the great news. This time, the wedding wasn't for my family or friends to offer their congratulations, comment on how beautiful I looked, or say how nice the wedding was; in fact, the wedding was simply the formal declaration of our commitment one to another. The wedding was nice, but I was focused on building a healthy marriage. After all, it's not about a finite ceremony—it's about a lifelong matrimony. God truly matured me, and I was grateful for a second chance.

Everyone was excited about our reunion—our daughter, our family, and especially Andre's mother, who had prayed on her sickbed for God to restore our marriage. We decided that this time our marriage would be different. Here are the seven factors that have led to our success so far:

1) We keep our priorities straight. I may have cheated on God before, prioritizing everything and everyone else above him, but I got it straight this time. Even my young daughter can tell you what my priorities are:

1. God

2. Spouse

3. Children

4. Work/my business

5. Family and community

Although we spend lots of time together as a family, we also spend uninterrupted time as husband and wife and as parent and child. This also gives each of us time alone so we can work on our individual activities, goals, and dreams. Most of the house is a communal area, but each family member also has his or her own "corner" of the house.

Given these priorities, I do my best to make sure that each one is handled properly before moving down the list. For example, I do my best not to work at home until I have first cooked dinner, spent time with my family, or read my daughter a bedtime story. In my business, I pride myself on being accessible to my business partners across the country; however, I turn off my cell phone after 9:30 PM so I can spend uninterrupted time with my family. Further, Andre and I go on frequent dates, and my daughter goes to her favorite babysitter's house. This provides an example for our daughter that my husband takes priority, even above her.

2) We live with our purpose in mind. Andre's role is to be the visionary, leader, and provider, just as Adam was to Eve; my role is to be his help mate (Gen. 2:18), that is, the perfect "fit" for my husband. We both submit to ourselves to God so that God is truly the head of our lives.

Wives, understand and support your husbands in ways that show your support for Christ. The husband provides leadership to his wife the way Christ does to his church, not by domineering but by cherishing. So, just as the church submits to Christ as he exercises such leadership, wives should likewise submit to their husbands. Husbands, go all out in your love for your wives, exactly as Christ did for the church—a love marked by giving, not getting. Christ's love makes the church whole. His words evoke her beauty. Everything he does and says is designed to bring the best out of her, dressing her in dazzling white silk, radiant with holiness. And that is how husbands ought to love their wives. They're really doing themselves a favor—since they're already "one" in marriage.

No one abuses his own body, does he? No, he feeds and pampers it. That's how Christ treats us, the church, since we are part of his body. And this is why a man leaves father and mother and cherishes his wife. No longer two, they become "one flesh." This is a huge mystery, and I don't pretend to understand it all. What is clearest to me is the way Christ treats the church. And this provides a good picture of how each husband is to treat his wife, loving himself in loving her, and how each wife is to honor her husband. (Eph. 5:22–33, The Message)

Throughout the Bible, it commands men to *love* their wives and for wives to *submit to* their husbands. This is an often contested scripture because most people, especially strong, independent women, may not like submitting to authority. I know—I've been one of them up until a few months ago. However, I realize that my husband loves me with agape love, he cherishes me, and I know that if he had to, he would die so that I could live. Therefore, I willingly submit to him in honor. I didn't always have this mindset, though. During my single years, I developed an independent woman's ego and determined that no man would ever tell *me* what to do. I'd have my own money, pay my own bills, make my own decisions, and live life how I wanted to live. Going from an independent woman to a submissive wife could have been a difficult transition to make, but I knew that it would be the only way for both Andre and I to fulfill the purpose designed for our lives in this marital relationship. So I humbled myself and gladly submitted to my husband.

3) We acknowledge that between the three of us— God, my husband, and me—nothing is lacking in

our lives. We both have strengths, and we both have weaknesses. However, it's amazing that my weaknesses are his strengths and vice versa! By openly admitting our weaknesses, shortcomings, and opportunities—and acknowledging the strengths that other possesses—it gives us an opportunity to lean on one another so we can accomplish more together than we could accomplish alone. This also liberates us from feeling insecure or inadequate for what we may lack as individuals.

For example, I like details while Andre likes the big picture. So I set up elaborate spreadsheets and formulas to manage our finances, while Andre looks at the trends in the market and within our portfolio. As another example, one of Andre's goals is to learn how to play the piano. As a lifelong pianist and former instructor, I'm now teaching Andre—and our daughter—how to play the piano. This is a great opportunity to make us even closer as a family and team. Together, with God, we lack for nothing.

4) We replace "yours and mine" with "ours." The notion of a fifty-fifty relationship is a fallacy. Although he's the designated cook of the family, there are times when Andre doesn't feel like cooking, so I may need to whip up dinner. (I know I'm a woman, but cooking isn't my gift. Plus, Andre was a cook in the military, so he's a professional!) Upon reflecting on my parents' marriage, I found lessons that Andre and I could apply to our relationship. My parents went through a period in which my father was laid off from his job and simultaneously lost his driving privileges because of his epilepsy. For years, my mother paid ridiculously high auto and health insurance premiums, and she was the only adult driver in the household for more than a decade. This had a tremendous impact on our family; my mother was stressed, and I imagine that my father felt emasculated because he wasn't able to fully provide for his family. So, it's not about fifty-fifty—or any other ratio—because there will never be a formula for how much each spouse consistently contributes to the relationship. Some days it might be fifty-fifty, but other times it could be ninety-ten. The bottom line is that it's about "ours, not yours." This is especially true because together, the two of us lack for nothing.

Even money is ours, jointly. This is probably unique from many married couples; after all, money is one of the biggest reasons couples have problems and is one of the biggest causes for divorce. We were determined that money would not cause any upsets in our new marriage. During our first marriage, we basically lived independently in the same household. We never merged our finances or our discussed financial assets. We decided the bills each of us would pay, and because Andre was committed to being a provider for his family, there were some days when he didn't have enough money to buy lunch, unbeknownst to me. Of course, he didn't reveal this to me at the time because I was so self-centered. But this time we were committed to doing things differently.

We decided that all money coming into the household would be *our* money and would go into one joint account. Money for all bills, investments, savings, and joint expenses were distributed from that account. This "ours, not yours" rule applies to all of our possessions, from money to cars to CDs. However, we also like having discretionary income to spend how we choose, so each month, both of us receive an equal allowance to spend, save, or invest any way we want. From this account, I buy clothes, pay for spa and pampering services like getting my hair and nails done, and oftentimes save up for larger purchases that I want to make.

We also defined our spending, savings, and credit policies—that is, what are the rules around which we will spend money, save money, and use credit. For example, one of our rules is that we may use our credit card to accrue airline miles, but we must pay it off in full every month so we don't waste money paying interest. Taking thirty minutes to define these policies helps us stay focused on the principles instead of making assumptions about one another and later becoming upset because of the other's decisions.

5) We develop mutual goals. One of the beautiful things about marriage is the power that lies in the team. Two can accomplish so much more than one person can accomplish alone. In Deuteronomy 32:30, it basically says that "one can chase 1,000, but with God's help, two can chase 10,000 enemies away!" That's means a husband-and-wife team have *ten times the power* than you'd have if you were alone. So in addition to our individual goals, we've developed mutual goals that yield even greater results than what we could accomplish alone.

Both Andre and I are visionaries. We love sharing new ideas with each other and talking about our goals together. After we agree on our goals, we both work together to make them happen. This vision also brings life into the relationship and gives us something new and exciting to focus on; after all, Proverbs 29:18 says, "Where there is no vision, the people perish." For example, Andre recently ran for public office, and we worked on his campaign together virtually every day for almost a year. Although he didn't win, we obtained valuable experience in working toward one common goal. We were focused on the same outcome, and the experience drew us closer together. At the beginning of the calendar year, we also identify the goals we have for the next three years, be it a financial goal, travel, learning a new skill or hobby, or growing our family.

6) We communicate honestly. From the beginning of our relationship, honesty has been the foundation of our relationship. This is one of the primary reasons why Andre and I could always trust each other, even through the most challenging times. Honest communication includes confessing our faults one to another and asking forgiveness, as I had done so many times during our separation. Confession and forgiveness create a clean slate and restore purity to our relationship. When we have conflict, the sooner we confess and forgive, the better our relationship is.

Honesty is also critical because we can't read each other's minds. Although this may seem obvious, when there's something on our minds, it's easy to hold it in.

Sure, sometimes we need to be quiet or be by ourselves, but when we feel that the other has wronged us and we fail to share our feelings with the other, it drives a wedge in between us. So, for the sake of our marriage—and to maintain a sense of inner balance and integrity—honest communication is essential. We also recognize and thank each other, even for the smallest of tasks, such as taking out the trash, washing the clothes, or opening the car door. In this way, we further demonstrate our love for one another.

7) We agape **each other.** "Trust steadily in God, hope unswervingly, love extravagantly" (1 Cor. 13:13, *The Message*). Finally and most importantly, life, marriage, and relationships are ultimately all about love, because if you don't have love, you don't have anything; and not just any kind of love—*agape* love. As spoken at our first wedding, 1 Corinthians 13 says it best:

> If I speak with human eloquence and angelic ecstasy but don't have love, I'm nothing but the creaking of a rusty gate.
>
> If I speak God's Word with power, revealing all his mysteries and making everything plain as day, and I have faith that says to a mountain, "Jump" and it jumps, but I don't love, I'm nothing.
>
> If I give everything I own to the poor and even go to the stake to be burned as a martyr, but I don't love, I've gotten nowhere. So, no matter

what I say, what I believe, and what I do, I'm
bankrupt without love.

Love never gives up,
Love cares more for others than for self.
Love doesn't want what it doesn't have.
Love doesn't strut
Doesn't have a swelled head,
Doesn't force itself on others,
Isn't always "me first,"
Doesn't fly off the handle,
Doesn't keep score of the sins of others,
Doesn't revel when others grovel,
Takes pleasure in the flowering of truth,
Puts up with anything,
Trusts God always,
Always looks for the best,
Never looks back,
But keeps going to the end.

Love never dies. Inspired speech will be over
some day; praying tongues will end; understanding will reach its limit. We know only a portion
of the truth, and what we say about God is always incomplete. But when the Complete ar-
rives, our incompletes will be cancelled.

When I was an infant at my mother's breast, I
gurgled and cooed like any infant. When I grew
up, I left those infant ways for good.

We don't see things clearly. We're squinting
in a fog, peering through a mist. But it won't be
long before the weather clears and the sun shines
bright! We'll see it all then, see it all as clearly

as God sees us, knowing him directly just as he knows us!

But for now, until that completeness, we have three things to do to lead us toward that consummation. Trust steadily in God, hope unswervingly, love extravagantly. And the best of the three is love.

Love is a beautiful thing. The resurrection of our marriage is truly a blessing from God, and there's no denying that I love Andre now more than ever, as I do our daughter. But they have to share my love because, more than anyone or anything, I love God—he will *always* be my first love.

Reflection Questions

1. Of the principles shares, which are most relevant for you? Why?

_____

_____

_____

_____

_____

2. What commitments will you make to your spouse and/or your significant other to deepen the relationship? What commitments will you make to yourself to prepare you for strong and healthy relationships with others, whether friendship or love?

_____

_____

_____

_____

_____

Author Biography

Kristin Harper is a speaker and business woman committed to helping people reach their full potential and creating healthy love relationships. She graduated with honors from Florida A&M University and currently lives in Cincinnati, Ohio. Kristin and her husband, Andre, travel together as seminar speakers, and are the proud parents of a daughter.